Child Support Kills

Montez DeCarlo

Contents

Child Support Kills: How To Avoid Becoming A Child Support Casualty

Foreword

Like taxes, child support is a necessary evil, but unfortunately for non-custodial parents who are usually men, the laws and tactics used to enforce child support is just as biased and destructive as the laws used to enforce the collection of delinquent taxes — even worse. Non-custodial parents have been persecuted by the court system since the inception of America and the formation of the universal judicial system. When a court case involves child support, adjudicators have persistently failed to choose common sense and reasonableness over irrationality and unbridled venom. The courts' broad discretion regarding child support, coupled with criminally biased child support enforcement policies, has created more casualties worldwide than all the historical crime waves combined.

There are no acceptable excuses for non-custodial parents who willingly decide to evade their financial responsibilities as parents, nor is it the intent of this book to make any excuses for them or to provide guidance for further evasion. Family laws are certainly necessary to make sure "deadbeat" parents are held responsible for co-creating a life and providing the basic necessities and resources to sustain that life. However, rather than approaching each child support case or situation objectively, adjudicators have consistently abused their discretion under the "best interest of the child" premise — which has significantly contributed to the systematic manufacturing of "deadbeat dads". It is this type of abuse that has destroyed bonds between parent and child, driven a great number of non-custodial parents to kill senselessly, or caused parents and children to commit suicide — hence the title of this book — *Child Support Kills*.

Child Support Kills highlights tragic events induced by inequitable child support laws and by the people who are sworn to accurately interpret and appropriately apply these laws. It is also designed to provide the reader guidance (not legal advice) on how to effectively challenge unlawful discretionary decisions made by district court judges presiding over child support court so that they can avoid becoming a criminal or mortality statistic — hence the subtitle — *How To Avoid Becoming A Child Support Casualty.*

Although there are several realities associated with child support, such as:

(This list isn't meant to be all inclusive)

- There are men that bounce from women to women--fertilizing their eggs at every stop (or should I say pop) and refusing to take financial responsibility when the seed develops into a child.

- There are men who become estranged from the mother of their children, and due to their dissatisfaction with the split, seek to punish the mother by ignoring or refusing to take financial responsibility for their children.

- There are women in our society looking for a free eighteen to twenty-one year ride by seeking to entrap unsuspecting men for the purpose of fathering bastard children for profit or a steady income.

- There are women who become estranged from the father of their children, and fueled by their anger over the split—whether it was based on mutuality or not, refuse visitation rights, move the children away from their fathers and or use the court system for vindication.

- There are mothers, fathers, and children living below the poverty line within the same household; however, if the parents separate or divorce, the fathers are held to a higher financial obligation to support their children; even more so than when they lived in the household. In fact, this is true for families that do not live below the poverty line, but it is more devastating to a father with less resources.

- There are fathers who are unaware of children that they have fathered, and after years of not knowing, they are brought into court just before the child's eighteenth birthday only to be taxed with an astronomical amount of back child support, which is usually based on their current salary.

- There are mothers who re-marry and forces the biological father out of the child's life by refusing visitation or not making the child accessible, only to drag the biological father into court years later (usually after they separate from their current husband or if they need to supplement their income) to claim back child support.

The ultimate reality for child support is that a child was conceived and as a result, will require adequate care and financial support to ensure it has the highest probability of surviving in the society in which it was born. The challenges, outcomes, and stigma associated with child support are universal; therefore, the injustice associated with child support enforcement is a universal dilemma as non-custodial parents are plagued with worldwide abuse of judicial discretion, which too often ends in senseless death.

There are always two sides of any story, but until adjudicators realize this fact and assess each child support case objectively, and legislators revamp the antiquated family (child support) laws to better promote and ensure unbiased and equal adjudication, deadbeat parents will continue to be manufactured, family values will continue to dissolve, and the inconspicuous victimization of innocent children will continue to escalate.

You can go to any library or book store to obtain a book on how to effectively navigate through the child support system or courts. However, *Child Support Kills* is the only book of its kind that illuminates the negative impact of a severely antiquated and unjust system. Rather than spoon feeding the reader subjective statistics or self-serving skewed data, *Child Support Kills* will introduce you to real stories and true accounts of murders and suicides that occurred because the fathers depicted felt that they had no alternative defense against draconian child support enforcement tactics or coping with unjust decisions made by the "family" court. Unfortunately, the fathers who are depicted in this book didn't have an opportunity to learn how to "force the hands of justice" prior to causing the demise of their children's mother, their innocent children, administrators or officers of the court, innocent bystanders, or taking their own lives.

For those non-custodial parents who are anticipating or currently engaged in a fight against child support injustice, *Child Support Kills* will serve as a valuable resource by revealing a proven strategy for tipping the scales of justice in their favor while facing an inequitable and biased child support system.

A System Ran Amuck

"Mr. Winslow, you are certainly a rarity in this court," exclaimed the judge. "In reviewing your case, the court acknowledges that you have successfully met your financial obligation for child support, and I might add, with no record of missing any payments. All non-custodial parents can learn from your commitment to doing the right thing for your child. As a result, this court hereby considers this case closed as to the matter of ongoing child support. However, in addressing your claim for overpayment in the amount of twenty thousand dollars, the Court finds that since there was no evidence presented to prove that your ex-wife intentionally received these funds for the purpose of personal gain or malice, we find that you were equally responsible for failing to introduce this matter to the court in a timely manner after the child reached the age of majority. Therefore, it would be unconscionable for this court to force Mrs. Winslow-Carter to return the alleged overpayment, especially when the intent of the payments was deemed to be in the best interest of the child. Your motion for the return of these funds is denied."

I was sitting in court that day and remember that after the judge rendered his decision, a murmur erupted throughout the courtroom that was so intense it felt as though an earthquake was brewing beneath my feet. I couldn't believe that I just witnessed a man, who obviously loved his child and was blessed with the means to pay a set amount of monthly support for a sustained period of time, get his spirit and wallet crushed by a stampede of injustice. The judge's discretionary and baseless ruling was definitely unfair and everyone in the courtroom knew it. Even Mr. Winslow's ex-wife knew it as she quickly blurted out "thank you, your honor," while trying to suppress the inevitable gluttonous laughter that was sure to come later.

Now, if Mr. Winslow was like most of the fathers depicted in this book, the outcome of this decision would have been nothing less than tragic. Although, his reaction was subdued, the visible lump in his throat and tear soaked eyes reflected a noble man trampled once again by an inequitable and painfully biased child support system; a system that obviously served as the final vindictive dagger for his ex-wife. I don't know the final outcome of their saga, but if it ended with Mrs. Winslow-Carter being found faced down in a pool of her own blood on the courthouse steps, the end result would have been included with the other child support induced tragedies highlighted in this book.

Sitting in court that day and witnessing what happened to Mr. Winslow, was my first experience with the often demonized child support system; a system that, prior to that day, I had heard so much about. Now I was about to be introduced to it as I sat behind my soon to be ex-wife, listening to her insidious banter with another so called scorned woman who was also preparing herself for the courtroom battle against an unsuspecting "deadbeat" dad. This day would unfortunately linger in the back of my mind for over twenty years as I fought my subsequent battles in child support court — battles that included multiple contempt hearings in multiple jurisdictions, over one thousand hours in child support court, several visits to debtors jail, bankruptcy, and ultimately, perfecting three successful appeals against unjust decisions made in child support court, two of which resulted in published opinions.

Yes, you read it right. I successfully appealed three separate court orders that were entered at the discretion of two seasoned child support judges;

one who eventually won a seat on the bench in Superior Court (while my appeal was pending) and the other who served as Chief Justice for the district. This was no small feat as I was up against an established local attorney that had over twenty-five years of experience, two seasoned judges, and my primary residence was over two hours outside of the jurisdiction where my cases were being adjudicated. Not to mention that I had no legal experience or experience with the appellate process, and had a very limited amount of funds. However, I prevailed by following the same guidance that I have elected to share with you in this book.

My rage against injustice and my determination to force the judges to follow the guidelines of the law and render a fair ruling in my case provided me with the adrenaline needed to turn a series of negative court events into subtle positive victories that could potentially benefit all non-custodial parents in the future. After I began the appellate process for my case, it immediately took on a whole new meaning — it wasn't just about justice for me anymore — it was about vindicating the injustice for all the struggling non-custodial fathers that came before me and setting a precedence for those that would follow.

Although, it is no secret that the child support laws are biased, outdated, and is in great need of reform, the injustice is often systematically perpetuated by those who are tasked with interpreting, applying, and enforcing the laws — t he child support judges, arbitrators, and overzealous lawyers who are tasked with child support enforcement. The problem is further exacerbated by the media's persistent negative portrayal of non-custodial parents, who are usually men.

Today, child support collection is big business for the local governments and private industry. Mom and pop outfits are springing up everywhere, claiming that they have a sure-shot system for making the "deadbeat dad" cough up the money they allegedly owe, which is often based on inaccurate information, uncontested claims, or unresolved matters of the court. As an enticement for their services, they place negative images and advertisements on billboards, television commercials, and other media outlets. These images typically depict men only, not "deadbeat moms", for which there are many.

In a 2004 article written by Jeffrey M. Leving, a renowned attorney who fights to ensure equal rights for fathers, and Glenn Sacks, a renowned activist for father's rights stated, in part:

"The government must now demand Justice and Equity in the state "Family" Courts, and promote the preservation of intact families by protecting the rights of children to be raised and supported---both financially and emotionally--, by BOTH parents, even after divorce. Federally subsidized collection agencies need to stop taking from the children what their RHETORIC pretends to protect.

The social fabric of society is built upon the strength of its family structure. Impoverishing and vilifying parents by misguided and flawed mercenary practices of government, joined at the hip to a multi-billion dollar divorce industry, is rapidly exsanguinating and killing the American family." Although, this statement is very relevant, the intent of *Child Support Kills* is not to belabor the obvious, but to introduce a strategy on how to fight fire with fire.

While father rights advocates are fighting the fight at the legislative level, non-custodial fathers can induce change at the grass roots level by challenging arbitrary and discretionary decisions made by child support law adjudicators by successfully perfecting the appellate process.

I am in no way professing that perfecting and winning an appeal in your case is an easy feat, but neither is changing federal policy. Just as we attempt to hold the lawmakers accountable by voting for and electing who we *think* are the right candidates for championing our cause, we must also hold the adjudicators accountable for properly interpreting and applying the laws. We have to attack from both ends.

Mr. Leving said it best in his book entitled "Father's Rights":

> *"Until truth, justice, compassion and common sense prevail more broadly and more consistently, a father facing exclusion from his children's lives must plan carefully, negotiate skillfully, and fight fiercely to assert and preserve natural rights and constitutionally guaranteed freedoms that most Americans take for granted."*

Unfortunately, at first glance, it appears that the non-custodial fathers highlighted in this book did not negotiate skillfully or fight fiercely enough to preserve their natural or legal rights in their respective cases. They ultimately became victims of a biased force that systematically drove them to their breaking points; which by the way is the same force and systematic pressures that victimized me for over twenty years until I finally stood up and challenged the purported powers that be.

There are a host of published books and articles on the Internet and on the market that are designed to assist fathers with dealing with unfortunate family matters such as divorce and child support as well as material designed to educate and provide insight into a system that has persecuted fathers for centuries. Reading Jeffrey M. Leving's book "Father's Rights" as well as John Phillip's article "The Father's Rights Survival Guide" (reprinted in this book by approval), will provide a non-custodial father with the information needed to help them wade through the trials and tribulations of dealing with a difficult ex-spouse and unjust court system. However, to complement their strategies, I have decided to share my experience with taking my child support case to the next level— the appellate court, which tipped the scales of justice in my favor.

Although the appellate process may seem daunting from the outset, it is not as difficult as it might seem or as most legal professionals would like to make it seem. Using the calculated and proven strategies outlined in this book, you are guaranteed to at least get your case before an appellate court, with a high probability of winning. The appellate process should be considered as the next viable step for proving to the opposition that you are serious about supporting your children and that you will not accept a baseless and unjust ruling entered against you by a judge that has most likely been biased by their own experiences, society, or public policy.

Why Appeal?

Most opponents of the appellate process regarding child support will argue that since the bulk of the damage is done in the lower courts, it leaves most non-custodial parents without enough resources, inspiration, or energy to continue the fight for minimal impact — not to mention the enormous cost involved with taking the fight to the next level. However, the fact is that child support matters are handled in the lowest branch of civil court and usually by people who are not judges, but arbitrators, magistrates, or in the case of Maryland — Masters. Although, orders or judgments entered by adjudicators that are not sitting judges must still be signed by a sitting judge to be considered final and effectual, most are often unfair, unlawful, and riddled with imperfection. If appealed properly, a non-custodial parent can level the playing field and induce justice in their case. The cost is minimal compared to the potential reward to be gained from winning an appeal. In most cases, the court costs are also refundable if you win.

The great Martin Luther King Jr. once said that "injustice anywhere is a threat to justice everywhere". Although appealing your case may not deliver you immediate relief if you win, it has the potential to immortalize justice for all future cases that may share the same subject matter as yours. If your appeal results in a "published" opinion, non-custodial parents who find themselves in the same situation as you will be able to legally reference your case in hopes of winning their case. A published opinion becomes case law, which is law based on judicial decision and precedent rather than on direct legal statutes.

The reality is, if you feel that an order or judgment entered by the judge seems unfair, there is a high probability that it is not only unfair, but unlawful.

A successful appeal will provide you much deserved vindication and may also allow you to recoup the costs for the underlining judgment such as lawyer fees, court fees, and other expenses used defending against the opposition in the underlining cause. Keep in mind that the subject matter for this book is child support, so the basis for your appeal shouldn't be focused on getting out of paying the required support, but to ensure decisions made by the lower courts are fair, equitable, and within the guidelines of the law.

Not only will winning your case on appeal set a legal precedence, it will force the judge and the lawyer for the opposition to stand up and take notice of what you have to say in your defense when you return to the lower court. When fighting for fairness during child support proceedings, there is nothing more gratifying than watching a judge or lawyer who belittled you in previous proceedings, eat their pride while being forced to render a decision in your favor based on an appellate court's mandate.

When an appellate court issues their mandate to the lower court, the judge has no other alternative but to adhere to their mandate. A mandate is a formal notice of a decision by a court of appeal; this notice is transmitted to the trial court and, when filed by the clerk of the trial court, constitutes the final judgment on the case, unless the appeal court has directed further proceedings in the trial court. The mandate is distinguished from the appeal court's opinion, which sets out the legal reasoning for its decision. In some jurisdictions the mandate is known as the *remittitur*.

Later in the book I will explain the different types of decisions that could be handed down by an appellate court and how those decisions could possibly affect your case, as well as present effective strategies and next steps you should take after an opinion from the appellate court is rendered. However, before you can even think about winning your case on appeal, you have to understand the proper strategies for preserving your case for appeal. The following section will introduce you to effective strategies designed to increase your chances for winning your case in the lower courts as well as serve as a guide to help you preserve and win your case in the appellate courts.

Unjustifiable Child Support Justified

Before I provide guidance for improving your chances on winning your case in the lower courts, I must first reveal the secret that no other book on the market has ever revealed regarding child support laws, child support enforcement, or child support court—a secret that even the bureaucrats and adjudicators worldwide don't want you to know about. As a bonus for reading this book, you are about to learn the most valuable strategy to avoiding the perils of an unjust child support system and being forced to pay child support. Take some time to grab a pen and write this down. Go ahead, I'll wait.

Are you ready? Here it is. The guaranteed method for avoiding child support and the infamous child support system is to never have children, or, accept the responsibility for caring for children that are not biologically yours – directly or indirectly. The former is obvious because if you are indeed responsible for the mutual conception of a child, then you are ultimately responsible for the financial support of that child until such time the child reaches the age of majority or either becomes statutorily emancipated. However, the latter is not so obvious, because if you accept responsibility for the financial support of a child for any sustainable period of time, even if you are not the biological parent or have not legally adopted the child, you can still be held ultimately responsible for the financial support of the child until he or she reaches the age of majority or becomes emancipated.

How can you be held legally responsible for the financial support of a child that is not biologically yours or one you have not legally adopted you ask? The answer is etched in case law that, by doctrine of equitable estoppel, the Court can hold you legally responsible. In <u>Farmer v. Gipson</u>, 201 Ky. 477, 257 S.W. 1, 2 (Ky. 1923), the Court's opinion provided one of the best clarifications on the doctrines of equitable estoppel as it applies to child support matters by stating that "the doctrine of equitable estoppel is predicated upon the theory that:

[w]here one has, by a course of conduct, with a full knowledge of the facts with reference to a particular right or title, induced another, in reliance upon such course of conduct, to act to his detriment, he will not thereafter be permitted in equity to assume a position or assert a title inconsistent with such course of conduct, and if he does he will be estopped to thus take advantage of his own wrong.

The doctrine is often stated in terms of the following factors: (1) Conduct, including acts, language and silence, amounting to a representation or concealment of material facts; (2) the estopped party is aware of these facts; (3) these facts are unknown to the other party; (4) the estopped party must act with the intention or expectation his conduct will be acted upon; and (5) the other party in fact relied on this conduct to his detriment.

In short, if you know that you are not the child's parent, but act in a manner where it is believed that you are the parent by your actions, then you cannot later attempt to forego your parental obligations to the child simply because you are no longer in a relationship with the child's mother.

To rub more salt into a festering wound, even if you were told that you were the parent of a child and it is later revealed that you are not the parent, you may still be obligated to pay child support as in the case of L.Y.T. v J.L.G., No. 920187, Erie County Court of Common Pleas, Pennsylvania (11/18/95) or the case of "Mr G." as it is so affectionately known throughout the Pennsylvania court system. The Pennsylvania Court held that "Mr. G." was estopped from denying support to the child he had mistakenly acknowledged as his because he had held himself out to be the father of, and had supported the child.

This decision rendered "Mr. G" an equitable parent who was helpless to deny the paternity of the child. The Court also found that "Mr. G" was not defrauded by "Ms. T" either before or after the child's birth since she told "Mr. G" about her dating another man.

The Court found the 1993 and 1995 blood tests that excluded "Mr. G" as the biological parent to be irrelevant.

The Court stated:

"Absent any overriding equities in favor of the putative father, such as fraud, the law cannot permit a party to renounce even an assumed duty of parentage when by doing so the innocent child would be victimized. Relying upon the representation of the parental relationship, a child naturally and normally extends his love and affection to the putative parent. The representation of parentage inevitably obscures the identity and whereabouts of the natural father, so that the child will be denied the love, affection and support of the natural father. As time wears on, the fiction of parentage reduces the likelihood that the child will ever have the opportunity of knowing or receiving the love of his natural father. While the law cannot prohibit the putative father from informing the child of their true relationship, it can prohibit him from employing the sanctions of the law to avoid the obligations which their assumed relationship would otherwise impose."

Similar cases have arisen in other states including Iowa, Arizona, Minnesota and California in recent years. However, there are many cases where men have been victimized by the mother and the Courts regarding paternity and have taken their cases to the next level in attempt to vindicate themselves and to eradicate the injustice that is so prevalent for most non-custodial parents, such as with the case of Carnell A. Smith of Georgia.

For 10 years Smith believed his former girlfriend, Toni W. Odom, when she said that he was the man who fathered her daughter. From 1989 to 1998 he voluntarily paid $375 a month in support of the little girl. However, in 2000 Smith acted on a hunch and got a DNA test. It showed he was not the child's father.

He unsuccessfully sought a new trial from DeKalb Superior Court Judge Edward A. Wheeler, who had presided over another paternity suit Odom brought. The state Court of Appeals denied his petition for discretionary appeal. Then the state Supreme Court denied him certiorari. But Smith would not stop until he had done everything he could do to resolve what he considered an injustice by the court's rulings. "They forced me to declare war on this child support system," he said. "They're telling me 'It's your fault for trusting her,' " he said.

Smith's petition stated that O.C.G.A. ' 19-7-40 grants superior courts the power to force a child's father to pay child support; however, the statute does not extend to non-parents. Smith wrote:

"Since petitioner is not a biological parent of the subject child, the Paternity Statutes do not vest the Superior Court with subject matter jurisdiction to order the non-parent Petitioner to pay child support," he wrote.

"The Court of Appeals or State Supreme Court should not be permitted to sub silentio ratify the trial court's jurisdictionally defective exercise of power to continue application of a mistaken child support order against a non-father."

Once he demonstrated to the court that he was not the child's father, Smith argued, the court should have been forced to admit it did not have subject matter jurisdiction over the case. "Granting a new trial is not discretionary in such circumstances, to rectify the mistaken previous judgments and orders; it is necessary in the interests of justice," Smith wrote. The Legislature addressed the issue during its last session by passing HB 369, setting out the procedure for someone like Smith to use conclusive scientific evidence to challenge a legal finding of paternity. The bill, which would become O.C.G.A. ' 19-7-53, directs the courts to grant petitioners relief "if genetic testing conclusively shows that the alleged father is not the biological father of the child and certain other conditions are met."

Those conditions include ensuring that the alleged father has not adopted the child, married the child's mother, or assumed responsibility for the child with the knowledge that he is not the child's biological father. If, as in Smith's case, a supposed father had no reason to disbelieve the child's mother, failure to challenge the legal finding would not bar him from reopening the case later if a DNA test contradicts her. The bill passed the House 163-0, and the Senate 45-5.

Although, Mr. Smith may never receive the relief that he fought so tirelessly for, others that come behind him who are faced with the same issues, will reap the benefit from his fight; which is also the intent of *Child Support Kills* i.e. to highlight the detrimental impact of antiquated child support laws as well as introduce more non-custodial parents to process of tipping the scales of justice in their favor.

The many accounts of injustice regarding child support issues or cases could easily fill any major metropolitan public library. Unfortunately, the overabundances of child support injustice do not make national or world news, which of course is a prerequisite today for motivating the masses to induce legislative change. The detrimental effects from unjust judicial decisions regarding child support cases are usually regionalized and buried in an obscure section of the local mid-week newspaper. My primary objective for *Child Support Kills* is to shine a spotlight on these issues in such a way that it might spark national action and new legislation geared to reforming the antiquated child support laws worldwide.

Winning the Battles while Preparing for the War

"Now the general who wins a battle makes many calculations in his temple ere the battle is fought. The general who loses a battle makes but few calculations beforehand. Thus do many calculations lead to victory and few calculations to defeat: how much more no calculation at all! It is by attention to this point that I can foresee who is likely to win or lose." - Sun Tsu

Translation: if you come to battle unprepared, be prepared to lose. The courtroom is the battlefield and for non-custodial parents, the opposing forces are the judges, lawyers, the custodial parent, and even the law. The deck is stacked against non-custodial parents from the moment the opposition files a motion for child support. From that point forward, non-custodial parents should always be prepared for battle.

In preparation for your case and upcoming court appearances, you should always think about the "what ifs". For example, what happens if you lose your case or if the court doesn't accept your position on certain issues and decides in favor of the opposition? What if you are forced to take your case to a higher court? Did you present your case and argument in such a way that all critical aspects of your case and evidence are preserved for presenting to the appellate court?

Preservation of issues and or facts in the lower court is the most important element to winning your case on appeal. If you didn't argue a certain point, present certain facts, or introduce certain evidence during the trial or hearing in the lower court, the appellate court will not accept them when you present your case on appeal. This is why it is very important for you to always be prepared for battle, so that you can ultimately when the war.

Let me be clear that my definition of winning the child support battle or war does not mean successfully circumventing the law for the purpose of avoiding your responsibility of paying child support. My definition of "winning the battle or war", as it pertains to child support cases, is the process of ensuring that the final decision of the court reflects fairness and justice for all parties involved; the custodial parent, the non-custodial parent, and the child or children.

Keep in mind that *"Child Support Kills"* was written to expose and address issues of the injustice surrounding child support, not divorce or custody issues, even though child support is often an outcome of divorce or custody proceedings; an outcome that can certainly be a contributing factor to inducing a detrimental reaction by a non-custodial parent.

Adherence to what I call the triple "P" approach, Preparation, Presentation, and Persistence, will not only increase your chances of success in the lower court, but will also increase your chances of getting your case heard and a favorable opinion rendered in an appellate court.

Preparation – being prepared takes significant effort, a certain degree of diligence, and mental tenacity on your part. The more complex your case is, the more research and preparation that is required. Your preparation begins when you receive the child support complaint and the Summons to appear in court.

Presentation – from your appearance to what you say and how you say it, is very critical to your success in court. As the old adage goes, "the first impression is the lasting impression." Therefore, if you want the judge to respect you and give you the benefit of the doubt, then dress appropriately.

In addition, learn proper court room etiquette by sitting in on other child support court cases prior to your court date; preferably court cases that are being heard by the same judge that's assigned to hear your case — if known.

Persistence – you should always respond to complaints and motions filed by the custodial parent. The worst thing you can do is not respond to a motion filed by the opposing party or not show up for a scheduled court date. By not responding or missing a court date, by default, you are affirming that the opposing party's argument or complaint has merit. Also, if your case is active and there appears to be a lull in the action or case, you should always take some time to review your case file just to make sure that an action wasn't filed without your knowledge.

Brown v. Brown, My Case Law and Precedential Reference

Brown v. Brown, 181 N.C. App. 333 (North Carolina Court of Appeals, January 2, 2007) - The Appellate Court found that the trial court erred in a civil contempt case based on child support arrearages by concluding that defendant was not entitled to recover attorney fees paid to purge himself of contempt. They reversed and remanded this portion of the order for entry of an order directing the $1,200 attorney fees to be paid into the office of the Clerk of Superior Court by the person or party who received it for disbursement to defendant, because it would be unconscionable to require defendant to pay for the services of plaintiff's attorney who improperly instituted contempt proceedings resulting in defendant's incarceration.

Brown v. Brown, 171 N.C. App. 358 (North Carolina Court of Appeals, July 5, 2005) - The Appellate Court found that the trial court erred by adjudicating the defendant in civil contempt of a 21 August 1996 judgment for child support arrears and vacated the judgment because: (1) N.C.G.S. § 50-13.4(f)(8) and (9) when read together provide that if a child support arrearage is reduced to a money judgment and the judgment provides for periodic payments, the judgment is enforceable by contempt proceedings; and (2) the civil judgment in this case was not enforceable by contempt proceedings when neither the 1996 judgment nor any subsequent orders of the North Carolina court required a specific unequivocal directive for defendant to pay child support on a certain schedule and/or by certain dates.

Brown v. Brown, Unpublished Opinion COA 04-1600 (North Carolina Court of Appeals, July 5, 2005) - the trial court was without authority to require the defendant to take the actions specified in a 8 September 2004 order requiring the payment of attorney fees and interest.

If you have not guessed it yet, the aforementioned cases are actual cases that I presented to the state appellant court Pro Se and won. No, I am not a lawyer, but I play one in real life. The two cases that resulted in Published Opinions are cited in North Carolina Trial Judges' Bench Book (Volume 1), which is a comprehensive legal reference on Family Law published by the University of North Carolina-Chapel Hill's School of Government. This reference book is being used in North Carolina's Judicial College courses to train district court judges on advanced and "hot topic" issues in child custody and support, post separation support and alimony, and equitable distribution. The gratification I get from seeing my cases cited in this courseware is indescribable because not only will the cases that I won on appeal serve as Case Law that can be used to help other non-custodial parents, but through formalized training, they are also being entrenched into the psyche of judges, which can also benefit non-custodial parents that will eventually come before them. This alone solidifies the fact that all of the blood, sweat, and tears I shed while fighting my injustice was not in vain and now serve a much larger purpose.

The events leading up to my multiple appeals and the subsequent favorable opinions are customary to what most non-custodial parents face with their child support cases. After being battered by a biased and unjust system for over twenty years, I decided enough was enough.
The primary purpose for my appeals was based on principle only, not denial, vindication, or an attempt to escape my financial responsibility for my children. At no time during the process did I deny the fact that I owed back child support.

In fact, during my last appeal I intentionally failed to present my case for the refund of child support or loss of wages caused by the illegal contempt order. My challenge was directed solely at the judicial system, namely the Family Court, and its precedential bias for custodial mothers' unlawful persecution of non-custodial fathers.

My story is like many of the non-custodial fathers that are currently fighting for justice against family courts around the world. I was a teenaged parent when I fathered my first child with my ex-wife. I wanted to do the right thing even with limited access to resources, so I married the mother of my child and joined the military. You know the story; we were young, rebellious, in popcorn love, and suffered from blind ambition.

After completing basic training, skills training, and serving a tour in Korea, we bought a home and moved in together with the ultimate goal of living happily ever after. Another child was conceived, bills increased, personalities clashed, secrets were revealed, immaturity exuded, fights ensued, and finally divorce became the only option for sanity. However, the divorce proceedings actually induced insanity and cultivated animosity, which rendered rationality an unattainable goal.

The court set the monthly child support obligation and ordered that my paycheck be garnished to ensure payment, which was not a problem for me at the time. The garnishment worked well for several years until I was a victim of a reduction in force from my job.
Struggling to find another job, I requested a modification to the existing child support order and received a fifty-dollar reduction. According to the Court, the minimal reduction was based on my "capacity to earn" and not my actual earnings.

Unfortunately, my "capacity to earn" was not communicated to the hundreds of employers that rejected my applications for employment, so needless to say, as I embarked on my multi-year quest for survival and self-sufficiency, my child support obligation remained the same, which led to insurmountable back child support. Although the children needs don't fluctuate based on the parent's income, governmental pressure on fathers living outside of the household to produce adequate income, are much more repressive than for fathers living in the household.

After three years of acquiring more experience and training in my field, I finally obtained a position that met the judge's "capacity to earn" requirement. By an order of the court, I resumed payment of my regular child support, to include a set amount toward back child support, which was also ordered by the Maryland court. By this time, my mother had passed away and I relocated to North Carolina to live in a home she left for me and my brother. Rather than seeking a modification to the payments for back child support in Maryland, my ex-wife hired an ambulance chasing lawyer to place a lien on the home I inherited from my mother with the intent to execute the judgment lien to get a lump sum payment for the back child support.

When I defeated the lawyer's attempts to execute the judgment, he unlawfully used the powers of contempt. I successfully appealed the contempt orders and through a subsequent appeal, received a reimbursement for the lawyer fees that I was forced to pay as a result of the fraudulent contempt procedures.

Although there were other hard fought triumphs against the judicial system during my ordeal, such as successfully defending against my ex-wife claims for interest on back child support after I won the appeals, at no time did the thought of killing myself, my children, or the mother of my children cross my mind. To maintain my sanity, I viewed my legal challenges as a contest of good versus evil. And, even though I lost some of the battles along the way, I used every resource and legal tactic available to a pro se litigant to ultimately win the war.

The reason I wrote this book was to share my experiences with those who are currently engaged in a child support battle with the family court, but do not have adequate resources to hire an attorney. This book is not to be used as a legal guide nor should be considered legal advice, but to be used as a resource for research if one should consider using the appellate process for their child support case.

The Appellate Process

If you don't like what happened at the end of a civil case in the lower court you can file an appeal with a higher court, which in most states is the Court of Appeals. This guidance is only for litigants who do not have a lawyer and are representing themselves in civil appeals.

An appeal is hard work, can take a lot of time, and can be very complicated. For the reasons mentioned, it is important to pay close attention to the Appellate Court's Rules regarding appellate procedures. The Rules control the whole appeal process and if you don't follow them you can ruin your own appeal and can be sanctioned by the Court. Don't expect special treatment just because you're representing yourself, everyone has to follow the Rules. This guidance does not provide legal advice, but it can provide the necessary information to help get your case in front of the Appellate Court. The Court of Appeals' staff will also help you as much as they can, but they cannot give you legal advice.

At the end of this guidance there is a list of the offices where you can file documents or can get information. I also included a glossary of legal terms.

REMEMBER, THE APPELLATE COURT'S RULES CONTROL AND YOU SHOULD ALWAYS FOLLOW THEM, NO MATTER WHAT IS INCLUDED IN THIS GUIDANCE.

THE "BASIC" STEPS

Step 1. How to File an Appeal.

1. When to Appeal? You have to file an appeal within a defined time period, usually 30 days after the lower Court enters a final order or judgment. Do not be late! The order must also be signed by a sitting Judge, not a Magistrate or Master.

2. What to File? A Notice of Appeal is what you need to file. The lower Clerk of Court's office has blank forms. You don't have to use these forms, but if you don't, then be sure that your Notice has the names of all the people who are bringing the appeal and that it says which order or judgment you're appealing. It is also a good practice to state for the record in open court that you will be appealing the Court's decision. This can also serve as valid notice, but be sure to check the Appellate Rules for your Court's jurisdiction.

3. Where to Appeal? You file your **Notice of Appeal** in the lower Clerk of Court's office, unless your case is a Landlord-Tenant case. If it is, then you file your Notice in the Landlord-Tenant Clerk's Office. By no means do you allow the Clerk sitting behind the desk tell you what you can or cannot file in your case. If you get resistance from the Clerk, simply ask them to date stamp your Notice and file it in your case jacket/folder. Be sure to get several initialed or signed "True Copies" of the date stamped Notice from the Clerk.

On my first appeal, the Clerk actually told me that the Notice of Appeal was not filed in their office, but I told her that she was not supposed to give me legal advice and to file the Notice as presented to her. She gave me a salty look and reluctantly date stamped the Notice and gave me a "True Copy". At that point, I did not care if she threw the original Notice in the trash because I had the "True Copy" stamped by her office. Be sure to serve or send all pleadings, complaints, or notices that you file in your case to the opposing party or their lawyer. Remember, to follow the Rules!

4. How Much does it cost? The cost varies depending on your jurisdiction and appellate Court Rules. In some instances and jurisdictions, you may be entitled to a refund of the fees or portion thereof, if you receive a favorable ruling in your case. If you cannot afford the costs, you can probably file a Motion to waive the Court Fees and Costs under the indigent premise. I was not aware of this when I filed my first appeal and was shocked when I received a refund from the Court after I won my appeal. Again, be sure to follow the Appellate Court Rules.

Step 2. The Record and Transcripts.

1. What is the Record? The Court of Appeals only looks to see if there was a mistake in the trial court. It does not hold a trial itself. But to see if something was wrong, the Court of Appeals needs to look at the record. The record is everything that was filed (Motions, Pleadings, Responses, Judgments, Orders, etc.) in the lower Court. In some jurisdictions, most of the required documents from the lower courts are automatically sent to the Court of Appeals.

2. What are Transcripts? Transcripts are a word-for-word copy of everything that was said at the trial or at a hearing. All Court cases are recorded! The transcripts can be important and you need to order them for the dates that you think that a mistake was made. The transcripts will become part of the Record.

3. When do you Order the Transcripts? You have to order transcripts within a set time period after you file your Notice of Appeal, so be sure to check the Rules.

4. Where do you Order the Transcripts? You order transcripts from the Court Reporter's office or the Clerk of Court.

5. Cost of the Transcripts? Transcripts can be expensive and you have to pay a deposit for them when you first order them and the rest when they're finished, unless you've been given permission to appeal without paying costs. If you have been given permission to appeal without paying the costs, then you don't need to order transcripts from the Court Reporter Division. Instead, you need to file a motion with the same lower Court judge who heard your case and ask him or her to order a transcript be prepared without you having to pay for it. You must also tell the judge what dates you need to have transcribed and why you need them. The Appeals Clerk will usually have blank motions forms you can use, just fill in what transcripts you need and explain why you need them. If this motion is denied, you have to pay for the transcripts. Almost all Court recordings are digital now, so the cost for the transcripts are more affordable these days.

Step 3. Briefs.

1. After the record is submitted based on the Rules, the Court of Appeals may issue an order telling you when to file your brief or there may be a time period for filing the brief after the record. I cannot stress this enough, please follow the Rules. You file one original and the required copies according to the Rules with the Clerk's Office at the **Court of Appeals** (NOT the lower Court Clerk of Court office). You must also send a copy of the brief to each appellee or their attorney. Be sure to

use certified mail when sending the brief to the appellee or their attorney. Remember this is war, so do not trust that your opponent will be honorable.

2. There may be a page limit for your brief. Check and adhere to the Rules.

3. After you file your brief, the appellee gets time to file a reply brief, usually 30 days. After the appellee files their reply brief, you can file a reply brief, usually you are allowed a shorter time period to file the reply brief, so check and adhere to the Rules.

Word of Advice: Take some time to review and research past Appeals and all the associated documents that were filed in your jurisdiction for cases similar to yours. Follow the briefing format and even reuse parts of the briefing that are relevant to your case (plagiarism is encouraged, especially if you are researching a winning case). These documents are in the public domain, so there should be no concerns about copyright infringement. If you cannot find copies on the Internet, take a trip to your Appellate Clerk of Court's office and pull a couple of old cases off the shelf to review and copy. It is best that you know the case number beforehand, but if you do not, simply ask the Clerk for assistance.

Step 4. Argument.

1. Once the briefs are all filed, the Court of Appeals will let you know if it wants to hear you make an argument in person. If it does, it will put your case on the Regular Calendar and tell you when the argument is scheduled. If the Court of Appeals does not want to hear an oral argument, it will put your case on the Summary Calendar for written Briefs.

2. If your case is on the Summary Calendar and you want to make an oral argument, you have to file a motion in the Court of Appeals asking for permission to argue. You have to file that motion within a set time period after you receive notice that your case is on the Summary Calendar. I do not recommend this, but if you were the captain of your debate club or an aspiring lawyer with law school credits, go for it.

Step 5. Decisions.

1. After the Court of Appeals reads everything and hears any argument, it will issue an opinion or order which decides if you win or lose. If you lose and you think the Court of Appeals made a mistake, you have three choices:

a. You can file a petition for rehearing at the Court of Appeals after the Court makes its decision. The petition goes back to the same judges who heard your case and it explains to them why you think they were wrong. Be sure to check and adhere to the Rules.

b. You can file a petition for rehearing en banc at the Court of Appeals after the Court makes its decision. This petition goes to all of the judges on the Court and asks them to hear your case all over again from the beginning.

Note: You can file both a petition for rehearing and a petition for rehearing en banc, but you have to file them together you can't wait to see if one type of petition is denied and then decide you're going to file the other type.

c. You can file a petition for writ of certiorari at the State or United States Supreme Court after the Court of Appeals makes its decision. This petition asks the Supreme Court to review the Court of Appeals' decision. If you file this petition, the Court of Appeals' Rules don't apply anymore and you must follow the Rules of the State or the U.S. Supreme Court.

IMPORTANT TIPS

1. Most of the time, you can't file an appeal for someone else like your spouse or a friend.

2. You can't appeal every decision the Superior Court makes right away, only final orders or judgments. The order or judgment almost always has to end the whole case against everyone before you can appeal. There are narrow exceptions to this rule, but check the Rules.

3. If you file an appeal don't think that means the person you've been ordered to pay can't start trying to collect or that you don't have to obey any other part of the lower Court's order. To stop the person from trying to collect or to protect yourself from having to do something you don't think you should have been ordered to do in the first place, you need to file a Motion for Stay Pending Appeal. The first place you file that is in the lower Court, with the same judge, and if he or she denies it, then you can file it in the Court of Appeals.
4. Follow the Rules for filing a Motion for Waiver of Prepayment of Court Fees and Costs.

5. You have to sign everything you file with the Court and put your address and phone number on it. You also have to keep the Court up to date on your address and phone number, let it

know if you move or they change. Again, review some old similar cases to get examples of the proper format.

6. You have to send a copy of anything you file to the appellees. You can do this by mail, by a private delivery service, by bringing it to them personally, or by faxing it to them if you both agree that faxing is ok.
You cannot fax anything to the Court of Appeals. You also have to attach a certificate of service to the filing. The rule of thumb is to send everything to the appellee by certified mail.

7. For your Brief, **remove all emotion and stick to the facts**. You will have several arguments that you will want to include in your Brief, so be sure to put your arguments in the order of strongest to weakest. To support your argument(s) only reference Published Opinions. These are Published Opinions from your state's Court of Appeals or Supreme Court. If there are no Published Opinions from your state's Court of Appeals or Supreme Court that can support your argument, you can reference Published Opinions from other states or the U.S. Supreme Court. Only use Unpublished Opinions to support your argument when no Publish Opinions exist.

As you can see, there are a lot of moving parts to filing an appeal, but the Rules provide the script necessary to succeed. Follow the script!

I must say that I was fortunate that my appeal case was in North Carolina, because North Carolina has digitized most, if not all, of its Court documents. It is very easy to navigate North Carolina's entire judicial system online. If you do not live in a state that has this type of online access, then you will need to do some leg work. Good Luck!

GLOSSARY

Here are some definitions of legal terms used with this guidance:

Appeal - this is what your case is called when you ask the Court of Appeals to review a decision made by the lower Court, which in some districts can be the District or Superior Court.

Appellant - this is the party who filed the appeal. It doesn't matter if they were the plaintiff or the defendant in the lower Court, either one can be an appellant in the Court of Appeals.

Appellee - this is the other party; the one who did not file the appeal. It doesn't matter who they were in the lower Court either, a defendant or a plaintiff can be an appellee.

Associate Judge - an Associate Judge is an active judge who was appointed by the President.

Brief - Your brief is a legal argument telling the Court why the lower Court's decision was wrong or why the judge abused his or her discretion.

Certificate of Service - this tells the Court how you served the other side and when you did it.

Civil case - this is a lawsuit between two parties that usually involves money.

Defendant - the person who was sued in the lower Court.

Dismiss or dismissed - means your case has been kicked out of court.

Final order - is a decision which resolves the whole case against all of the parties in the lower Court.

Judgment - is a final order that tells one person to pay another person some money or to do something specific.

Magistrate or Master Judge - is a judge who was appointed by the Superior Court Board of Judges to help Associate Judges with their work. Their decisions and orders are not final until after they are reviewed by an Associate Judge.

Motion - this is what you file when you want to ask the court to do something.

Opinion - this is a written explanation from the Court that says why you won or lost your appeal.

Opposition or response - is the filing that is made in response to a motion.

Party - anybody who participated in the case in the lower Court or in the Court of Appeals.

Plaintiff - the person who filed the lawsuit in the lower Court.

Published Opinion – are referred to as Case Law and is one of the major sources of law in common law legal systems.

Record - is everything in the lower Court case file and any transcripts that are prepared.

Regular Calendar - a list of cases that the Court of Appeals wants to hear oral argument on.

Reply brief - is a brief that an appellant can file in response to the appellee's brief.

Service - this means you have made sure your opponent has been sent or given a copy of anything you file in the court.

Summary Calendar - is a list of the cases that the Court of Appeals will not hear oral argument on.

US State Appellate Courts Online

Alabama - http://www.judicial.state.al.us/civil.cfm

Alaska - http://www.state.ak.us/courts/appcts.htm

Arizona - http://www.cofad1.state.az.us

Arkansas - http://courts.state.ar.us/courts/ca.html

California -
http://www.courtinfo.ca.gov/courts/courtsofappeal

Colorado - http://www.courts.state.co.us/coa/coaindex.htm

Connecticut -
http://www.jud.state.ct.us/external/supapp/Default.htm

Delaware -
http://courts.delaware.gov/Courts/Supreme%20Court

District of Columbia -
http://www.dcappeals.gov/dccourts/appeals/index.jsp

Florida -
http://www.flcourts.org/courts/circuit/circuit.shtml

Georgia - http://www.gaappeals.us

Guam - http://www.guamsupremecourt.com

Hawaii - http://www.courts.state.hi.us

Idaho - http://www.isc.idaho.gov

Illinois -
http://www.state.il.us/court/AppellateCourt/default.asp

Indiana - http://www.in.gov/judiciary/appeals/index.html

Iowa - http://www.judicial.state.ia.us/Court_of_Appeals

Kansas - http://www.kscourts.org/ctapp

Kentucky - http://courts.ky.gov/courts/courtofappeals

Louisiana - http://www.lasc.org/links.asp#CourtsofAppeal

Maine -
http://www.courts.state.me.us/mainecourts/supreme/index
.html

Maryland-
http://www.courts.state.md.us/coappeals/index.html

Massachusetts -
http://www.mass.gov/courts/courtsandjudges/courts/appe
alscourt/index.html

Michigan - http://courtofappeals.mijud.net
Minnesota - http://www.courts.state.mn.us/?page=551
Mississippi -
http://www.ncsconline.org/D_KIS/CourtWebSites/CtWeb_
MSappeals.htm
Missouri - http://www.courts.mo.gov/page.asp?id=261
Montana - http://courts.mt.gov/supreme/default.asp
Nebraska - http://www.supremecourt.ne.gov/appeals-
court/index.shtml?sub2
Nevada - http://www.nvsupremecourt.us
New Hampshire -
http://www.courts.state.nh.us/supreme/index.htm
New Jersey -
http://www.judiciary.state.nj.us/appdiv/index.htm
New Mexico - http://coa.nmcourts.com
New York - http://www.courts.state.ny.us/ctapps
North Carolina -
http://www.nccourts.org/Courts/Appellate/Appeal/Defaul
t.asp
North Dakota - http://www.court.state.nd.us
Ohio - http://www.sconet.state.oh.us/District_Courts
Oklahoma -
http://www.oscn.net/oscn/schome/civilappeals.htm
Oregon - http://www.ojd.state.or.us/courts/coa/index.htm
Pennsylvania -
http://www.courts.state.pa.us/Index/Supreme/indexSupre
me.asp
Puerto Rico - http://www.tribunalpr.org
Rhode Island -
http://www.courts.state.ri.us/supreme/defaultsupreme.htm
South Carolina -
http://www.judicial.state.sc.us/appeals/index.cfm
South Dakota - http://www.sdjudicial.com
Tennessee -
http://www.tsc.state.tn.us/geninfo/courts/AppellateCourts.
htm

Texas - http://www.courts.state.tx.us/courts/coa.asp

Utah - http://www.utcourts.gov/courts/appell

Vermont - http://www.vermontjudiciary.org/courts/supreme/index.htm

Virginia - http://www.courts.state.va.us/cav/home.html

Virgin Islands - http://www.visuperiorcourt.org

Washington - http://www.courts.wa.gov/court_dir/orgs/120.html

West Virginia - http://www.state.wv.us/wvsca

Wisconsin - http://www.wicourts.gov/about/organization/appeals/index.htm

Wyoming - http://www.courts.state.wy.us/SupremeCourtClerksOffice.aspx

Child Support Casualties

(Reference: Various News Sources)

The Most Famous Child Support Killer Case:

November 1999

Rae Carruth, Carolina Panthers' star Wide Receiver, arranged the killing of Cherica Adams and his unborn baby in Charlotte, NC because he did not want to pay child support. Cherica died from the gunman's attack, but not before identifying Rae as the culprit. The baby lived. Since Rae didn't pull the trigger, he was sentenced to 18-24 years in prison.

Man murdered 'to avoid child support'
July 27, 2004 - 9:53AM

A man has been indicted for allegedly pushing his four-year-old daughter to her death from a cliff 36 metres above the Pacific Ocean so he wouldn't have to pay child support. Cameron John Brown, 42, pleaded not guilty to the charge of murdering Lauren Key. The district attorney's office said prosecutors will decide later whether they intend to seek the death penalty.
He has been jailed since his arrest in November, when charges were initially filed in the case. The indictment, unsealed today, supersedes the earlier charges and means the case can proceed to trial without a preliminary hearing.
The little girl died on November 8, 2000, on Palos Verdes Peninsula, where Brown claimed she had slipped as they hiked to a spot high above the ocean called Inspiration Point, officials said.

June 2004

Pennsylvania authorities say 18-year-old Gregory Rowe murdered his 7-month-old daughter and the infant's teenage mother — one day before their child support hearing…

Texas Gunman Was Angry Over Child Support Dispute
Police: 2 Dead, 4 Hurt Outside Tyler, Texas, Courthouse
February 2005

TYLER, Texas -- A man being sued for child support went on a shooting rampage in East Texas that left the gunman and two victims dead, and four people wounded.

David Hernandez Arroyo Sr., 43 -- a man with a history of spousal abuse -- shot and killed his ex-wife on the Smith County Courthouse steps, then sprayed the courthouse square with deadly gunfire, police said.
He got away from the courthouse but died in a shootout with police nearly 100 miles east of Dallas. After a brief chase, police said they rammed Arroyo's SUV and the gunman stepped out, guns blazing. He was killed by police gunfire.

He was apparently upset over a child support dispute with his ex-wife and started shooting just minutes before his court hearing.

April 2007

James H. Stewart, 24, died from two gunshots to his back after the officers tried to arrest him for failing to return to Northampton County Prison after a work-release assignment. He had been jailed for failing to make **child support** payments. He was found at his sisters by two police officers.

The officers ordered him to stand, asked his name and checked his identifying tattoos. When they told Stewart to turn around, he took a box cutter from his belt and "tried to stab himself." One of the officers wrestled the box cutter away and threw it to the floor. As Stewart stood with his back to the officers and arms to his sides, Moll shot him. Stewart fell to his knees, and Moll shot him again in the back. Stewart dropped to the floor, where he lay dying in a pool of blood. When Wilcox yelled at Moll, asking what he was doing, Moll replied, "I don't know! I don't know!"

Police Shoot Man in Child Support Case
Naples, Florida
February 1996

Officers showed up to arrest Allen T. Powell for being behind in his support payments. When Powell cited his Constitutional rights and refused to be taken, the officers sprayed him with Cap-Stun, a Mace-like substance.

Powell took one of the officers' flashlights to defend himself, striking both officers. The officers then opened fire, shooting Powell 5 times in the chest and abdomen – killing him instantly.

Killing Spree Triggered by Child Support Errors
April 2006

Herbert Chalmers Jr. claimed that he was not the father of the three children for whom he was making child support payments. His employer told Chalmers to contest the issue with the state but that the wage garnishments would continue. Chalmers killed four women (including his employer's wife and daughter), and then himself.

State officials later admit that they were overcharging the man by five times as much as he actually owed, however, the paternity issue wasn't addressed.

Man Who Killed Ex-Wife With Bomb Sentenced To Life
November 2003

JACKSONVILLE, Fla. -- Convicted killer William Jarvis was sentenced to life without parole Friday morning for the bombing death of his ex-wife, Lillian.

Last month, Jarvis was found guilty of first-degree murder in the January 2001 bombing of his ex-wife's parents' home with a bomb wrapped like a Christmas present. The jury recommended life in prison.

The former air traffic controller from Hilliard also received three other life sentences on charges resulting from the fire and injuries of other family members.

During the sentencing hearing, Jarvis maintained his innocence. Prosecutors have said that Jarvis murdered her because he didn't want to pay alimony or child support.

August 17, 1992

Robert Earl Carter decided to kill his former girlfriend, Lisa Davis, and Jason, Lisa and his 4-year-old son. He armed himself with a .22 caliber pistol, a knife and a hammer and drove to her home in Somerville, Texas. Lisa lived with her mother and sisters but that night, she was not at home. Her mother, Bobby Joyce Davis, was there with her other daughter, Nicole, her grandchildren, Brittany and Lea'Erin and Lisa's two children, Jason and D'Nitra. He killed them all.

Carter was under pressure from Lisa to increase the child support for their son, Jason. He was already supporting his wife, Theresa, their son, Ryan, as well as the child support for Jason. He was a 27-year-old prison guard, employed at the Texas Department of Corrections on a low but adequate wage. Anger over being asked to increase the child support payment does not qualify as sufficient explanation for what happened, but it is the only motive that has been suggested.

Man killed at court was upset over child support
June 2005

Perry Manley didn't want to pay child support, and the seeming unfairness of a system that hounded him to turn over his hard-earned cash to his ex-wife had made him angry and obsessed over the past 15 years.
Manley had written and talked about the topic *ad nauseam*. He had filed no fewer than five lawsuits, and had joined others supporting the rights of fathers as noncustodial parents. Being required to pay child support for his three children, Manley claimed, was a form of involuntary servitude, where a man is forced to work to support a child he is not responsible for raising. In recent years, his writings and actions showed him to be increasingly bitter.
In the end, his obsession is apparently what got him killed, in what friends believe was a last-ditch effort to draw attention to his cause.
Manley was shot to death yesterday, the day after Father's Day, by two Seattle police officers inside the secure foyer of the federal courthouse. In one hand, he clutched a defused fragmentation grenade.

3-Year-Old Girl Killed Over Child Support
January 2005

DETROIT -- The mother of a 3-year-old girl who was killed in a rampage at a local day-care center took the stand Monday in the murder trial for the child's father.

Prosecuting attorney Lisa Linsey said in her opening argument that Bernard Kelly beat his 3-year-old daughter to death that day because he no longer wanted to support her financially.

"The defendant, Bernard Kelly, executed 3-year-old Stephanie Belue and her only crime was that she was simply born," said Lindsey.

Missouri
August 2000

Kimber Edwards hires a hitman to kill his ex-wife Kimberly Cantrell because of the increased pressure to pay back child support. She died in her home from two gunshots to the head.

Randy Orville Brouse, 33, of Illinois, when jailed for felony failure to pay child support, hung himself on July 21, 2003. Prior to his death, he was one of 50 Hillsdale County's "Most Wanted". All are alleged to be dangerous and wanted "for serious and often violent crimes". In fact, more than 60% are wanted only for failure to pay child support. The Hillsdale's dangerous, "Most Wanted" list of those unable to pay the court ordered amount of child support consists of 32 people of the 51 Most Wanted.

Trevor Goddard, 37, of North Hollywood, California, committed suicide on June 8, 2003. Goddard was at the height of his career. His credits include, Mortal Kombat, Men of War, JAG, Deep Rising, Gone in 60 Seconds, and the recently released, Pirates of the Caribbean. Few know that Trevor was in the middle of a divorce and finding out just what that means to a loving father. There were many articles on his death, but, only one mentioned his pending divorce.

Robert R Steadman, 33, of Sewickley Township, Pennsylvania, hung himself in April, 2003 during his second imprisonment for failure to pay child support. Since Robert was only one sentence of the story dealing with suicide watch policy changing for that prison, it is unknown if this second jailing was a 90 day recycle. The recycle is a jail term of 90 days. After 90 days, the prisoner is released, only to be greeted by another incarceration for failure to pay child support for 90 days and the cycle is continued.

Reinaldo Rivera, 25, of New Jersey was jailed for failure to pay child support. He hung himself with a sheet after one week in jail in April, 2003.

Derrick K. Miller, 43, of San Diego, California, walked up the steps courthouse steps to the San Diego family court's security guard on January 7, 2002. Miller had recently been judged to pay support he obviously did not have. While holding his divorce papers in one hand and pulling a pistol in the other, he told the guard, "You did this to me!" Derrick quickly pulled the trigger, on the only option left to him and many other fathers, sending a bullet through his head and died.

Carl Tarzwell, Jr., 37, was arrested on June 20, 2001, for failing to pay child support. Carl hung himself within a few hours of being jailed. Carl's death was revealed in a November, 2001, article dealing with excessive suicides in prison.

James Gunter, 45, an emergency services police officer, described as "one of those steely, go-to guys, a natural in a crisis", took his life on the third try while incarcerated for the third time. James was arrested for failing to pay child support and failing to stay away from his ex-wife. Gunter's daughter stated, "He couldn't stand to be away from his kids." James Gunter found peace on September 15, 2000. It was not until March 24, 2002 that James' story became noted by the press in a story about jails being at fault for lack of care in suicides.

Randy Johnson, 34, of Sommerset, Kentucky hung himself on the second day of his incarceration for felony failure to pay child support in January, 2001. He could have been sentenced to 5 years. Johnson worked for the Sugar Shack making donuts. His employer said he was trying to lead a new life. Johnson's story is revealed in an article about suicides in Boyle County prison.

Darren Bruce White, 34, of B.C., Canada, killed himself sometime between March 12, 2000 and March 17, 2000, when his body was found. Darren's suicide came shortly after a court ruling he was **capable**, something US family courts are also known to do as attested by the author in his personal experience, of paying $2,071 a month in support.

David Guinn, 38, incarcerated for probation violations and was behind on his child support, hung himself on November, 1998.

James A. Poore, 33, of Bristol, Tennessee, arrested for failing to appear at a child custody hearing, found a shotgun while on a work release program and promptly blew a hole in his chest in March, 1999.

Kenneth Taylor, 40, of Nebraska, hung himself while jailed for felony child support in November, 1999.

4 Women Killed in Child Support Office
October 1992

Four women and their killer died when 50-year-old John T. Miller walked into local child support office with a 9-millimeter handgun and shot one after the other, pausing once to tell a woman working in a nearby office that she could leave. Afterward, he calmly told deputies that he had "hurt everyone I came here to hurt." Then he held the gun to his right temple and pulled the trigger.

1997

Coleman Johnson planted a pipe bomb that killed his ex-girlfriend, who was eight months pregnant, to avoid the child support that he would have to pay.

Charges murder, arson in 2 deaths.
July 2006

A **Detroit man** who police say **killed** his daughter and girlfriend because he did not want to pay **child support** and wanted to keep their relationship hidden was charged Wednesday with murder and **arson** in their deaths. Jimmie Reed Jr., 30, was arraigned in 50th District Court in Pontiac on open murder and **arson** charges in the death of Markeda Byas, 31, and on felony murder and **arson** charges in the death of Arctavia Reed, who was 2 months old.

Family blames child support payments for nurse's suicide
July 2005

Leigh Eglon, 41, a father of three, killed himself because he could not afford child support payments after his divorce in 2001; Manchester Coroner's Court was told by his family. The operating theatre nurse, who earned up to pounds 500 a week, was once left with pounds 10 to support himself, the inquest heard.

Child Support related Deaths in the United Kingdom:

Angela Jones
Daily Express 19 January 1994

The controversial Child Support Agency came under fresh fire last night after another family tragedy.

Mother-of-two Angela Jones was stabbed to death and her estranged husband Terry tried to kill himself.

Detectives questioning him at his hospital bedside yesterday wanted to know if the drama was linked in any way with a massive maintenance demand he had received from the CSA 24 hours earlier.

And there were new demands for a tougher clampdown on the agency's operations.

Ken Mayo, of the National campaign for Fair Maintenance, said: "The Government must act; Ministers are presiding over a growing catalogue of tragedy. The CSA should be renamed the Child Orphaning Agency. Thousands of people in second marriages are being driven to the edge by it."

Last year father-of-two Graham Clay, 30, a stately home curator hanged himself after the CSA trebled his payments. He left a note saying: "No one will listen. I did my best. All I got was pain".

In the latest incident 40-year-old Mrs Jones was found dead with six stab wounds in the kitchen of her home in Woodham Terrace, Barry, Glamorgan. Neighbours said her body was discovered by 12-year-old son Huw who screamed: "Mummy's dead."

Huw's grandmother Violet Edwards opened the garage door and saw Mr Jones, 41, slumped in his fume-filled car. His pockets were full of press cuttings highlighting the injustices of the agency. As he was recovering last night, friends said the £16,000-a-year company fire officer loved Huw and daughter Karla, six, but could not afford higher maintenance.

The CSA said: "we are aware of this case but cannot comment."

Mr Jones, married for 20 years, left his wife after an affair five months ago. His mother said: "They were getting divorced." His close friend Gordon Roberts added: "He would go to the end of the earth for his children. There was never any question of him abandoning them so I don't understand why the CSA was chasing him."

Angela's friend Bridget Hall said: "Terry is a dutiful father. He takes the youngsters out. He bought a flat 10 miles away in Whitchurch but I don't think the other woman has moved in." The CSA was recently accused of ignoring guidelines by telling divorced mothers how much second wives earn.

In December, after protests from MPs, the Agency's rules were changed allowing maintenance payments to be phased in over a two-year period

Brian Gorton
Daily Mirror 18 March 1994

In November, jobless dad Brian Gorton, 42, of Spalding, Lincolnshire, hanged himself after a court doubled his £100 a month payments to his ex-wife.

Derek Atkin
Daily Express 25 March 1994

A 37-year-old civilian working with Humberside police was found dead in his car shortly after the CSA contacted him. A hose pipe was attached to the exhaust.

His mother, Mrs June Atkin, 56, said: "He had been having terrible trouble with the CSA. He told me they were trying to take very penny."

But this week CSA chief executive Ros Hepplewhite denied that her agency had driven the fathers to take their own lives. She said: "I really do not think that the agency is to blame."

James McKay
Daily Express 25 March 1994

So far five fathers have committed suicide because they could not afford to pay huge demands, say protesters.
The latest victim was 35-year-old Jim Mckay who was found hanged in his council house in Rutherglen, Glasgow, on Saturday.

He had been told to hand over all but £12 of his £39.90 unemployment and sickness benefit to support his two young children.

Mr McKay's brother, Edward, 39, said: "It is all because he was hounded by the CSA."

Jacqueline Quinn, mother of six-year-old Stacey and James, two, said she and Mr McKay were planning to get back together.

She added: "I have lost my man and my children have lost their father for the sake of a few pounds."

Graeme Lowe
Daily Express 25 March 1994

Graeme Lowe, a 38-year-old technician, gassed himself in his car in Sunderland when he was unable to afford new agency demands.

His father Robert branded the CSA 'a disgrace'.

Sean Lyford-Smith
Today 29 April 1994

A young father hanged himself after the Child Support Agency said his maintenance payments were to be trebled, an inquest heard yesterday.

A CSA letter found at the flat of Sean Lyford-Smith said his £10 a week voluntary payment was going up to £27.75 – and there were arrears of £578.

West Somerset coroner Michael Rose said the letter would have had a frightening effect on the 23-year-old computer operator.

He is to 'make representations' to the agency, after hearing how Mr Lyford-Smith was later reassessed to pay ex-girlfriend Joanne Patey only £12.85 a week for their four-year-old daughter Maria.

Recording a verdict of suicide, the Coroner said: "I can't help wondering whether I would be sitting here today if the right figures had been arrived at earlier."

A letter confirming the reduction in his payments and arrears would have been sent to Mr Lyford-Smith in March but he was dead.

Stephen Jackson
Daily Mirror 7 May 1994

A verdict of suicide was recorded in November on Birmingham prison worker, Stephen Jackson.

May of this year Stephen received a CSA demand for £2,500 maintenance arrears and shortly afterwards he took an overdose of sleeping tablets. At the inquest his brave mother, Mrs Lorna Jackson, said: "... the letter from the CSA was on the top of the pile of suicide notes. I feel very bitter."

John Spellar MP (Labour, Warley West) said: "The CSA appears to have no understanding of the devastating effect that massive demands for arrears can have."

The letters Stephen left were addressed to John Major, his mother and father and his children and referred to the anguish he felt at the way the CSA was treating him.
Goolan Hassen
Daily Mail 18 May 1994

A coroner blamed a **mistake** by the CSA yesterday for triggering a father's death from an overdose of drink and drugs.

A maintenance demand for £3,000 – three times higher than it should have been – was found beside the body of hospital nurse Goolan Hassen, 55.

"It was the letter that proved the trigger that led to his death," said coroner David Wadman, who recorded a suicide verdict. "It is a sorry state of affairs. Had the true situation been put to him, who knows what would have been?"

Mauritius-born Mr Hassen had split from his wife Brenda, a GP's receptionist, but they agreed not to involve the CSA as he paid £9,000-a-year for the private education of his nine-year-old son and daughter of 13, an inquest heard at Eastbourne, Sussex.

The £22,000-a-year night nurse at Eastbourne Hospital lived in a rented flat and is understood to have taken on day jobs to pay for his children's schooling.

The CSA became involved when Mrs Hassen was unemployed for two months and claimed income support. CSA official Colin Oudot said the agency was not required to take into account Mr Hassen's contribution for schooling. The letter was generated by computer and sent out automatically but should have demanded only £1,000.

Peter Ayres
The Independent 29 May 1994

Peter Ayres, an engineer from Longthorpe in Gloucestershire apparently decided he could take no more, having received the usual 'pay up or else' threatening letters from the CSA. It's reported that he wired up his wrists to a high voltage circuit, threw a switch and electrocuted himself.

Alan Creeton
Daily Telegraph 4 August 1994

A married executive who was secretly paying maintenance for an illegitimate baby killed himself after receiving a letter from the Child Support Agency and fearing he was about to be exposed, a Southampton inquest heard yesterday.

Mr Alan Creeton, 41, drove to a remote part of the New Forest and gassed himself inside his car the day after he received a CSA assessment and realised his wife, Christine, would find out about the baby, born as a result of a brief and 'purely sexual' affair.

He had been paying £20 a week to the baby's mother, but the CSA became involved last month and wrote to Mr Creeton, an area manager for a hotel chain, the inquest heard. His wife said later: "He died to keep a secret."

On the day he received the letter, he sought immediate legal advice on the payments and whether he could keep the matter from his wife. But when he was told that all other CSA documents would be sent to his home, he told a trainee legal executive: "Maybe I should commit suicide."

The next day he went to see his wife at a sports centre where she worked and his teenage daughter, Stephanie, before leaving a farewell letter on a coffee table at their home in Ladysmith, Christchurch, Dorset, adding: "The last two years have been hell. By the time you read this, I will be dead."

Mrs Creeton, who had often quizzed him on why they never had enough money for a holiday, told the inquest that she knew he had been having an affair with a colleague called April Gray, but knew nothing of the baby which resulted from another relationship.

"I was not aware of any problem that would have led him to kill himself," she told Mr Christopher Hodgkinson, deputy coroner.

Miss Louise Powell, the trainee legal executive Mr Creeton consulted on July 25, said he told her he had been named as the father of a child by the CSA.

"He asked how much he would have to pay," said Miss Powell. "He took away a self-assessment form. He'd asked the woman to have an abortion, but she had not. His records showed payments to her of £20 a week over the last year.

"He asked if he could keep it from his wife, but I told him that the CSA would send the details to his home. As he left my office, he said maybe he should commit suicide. I said that nothing was that bad."

When police found Mr Creeton's body in his car, there were photographs of his wife and daughter on the passenger seat. Mr Hodgkinson recorded a verdict of suicide.

Malcolm Taylor
The Independent 6 August 1994

A loving husband died in his fume-filled car after he was forced to leave his second wife because of demands from the Child Support Agency, an inquest heard yesterday.

The inquest at Cannock, Staffs, was told that Mr Malcolm Taylor, 34, formerly of Coalpit Lane, Brereton, Staffs, became depressed after the CSA started to investigate his affairs and bombarded him with letters about his first wife.

He was found dead in his car surrounded by letters from the CSA. A hose pipe led from the exhaust into the vehicle. His second wife, Mrs Lyn Taylor, said in a statement that she and her husband had enjoyed a happy marriage until he started to receive letters from the CSA about nine weeks before his death. The letters had worried and depressed him.

"Eventually, they suggested it was in his interest to leave his second wife and live elsewhere so that his state benefits would not be affected. He agreed to do this, but became increasingly depressed."

Mr Reginald Browning, the South Staffordshire Coroner, recorded an open verdict after being told that Mr Taylor had appeared to be his usual self shortly before his death. Mr Browning said there was no evidence as to what was in his mind at the time.

A spokesman for the CSA said: "The reasons why anyone takes his own life are complex. It is not appropriate for the CSA to comment on individual cases."

Linda Greener
Daily Telegraph 3 September 1994

Miss Linda Greener, 30, a business studies student of Cheadle, Staffs, died from a drugs overdose in July 1994. Mr Stephen Baldwin, her common-law husband, blamed the CSA for hounding him. He said: "She seemed to blame herself for our problem because she was not out earning money."

Angela Jenkinson
Vincent Hand
The Times, 19 September 1994

Detective Constable Vincent Hand, married and aged 31, strangled his seven months pregnant mistress, Angela Jenkinson and then gassed himself in his own car. According to reports the tragedy occurred following Ms Jenkinson's threat to contact the CSA after the baby was born. Later DNA testing revealed that Hand was not in fact the father of the child.

This is believed to be the second occasion where murder (or at least attempted murder) and a suicide have occurred simultaneously as a result of threatened CSA involvement.

Steve Willey
Daily Mail 28 October 1994

A fireman involved in a long and bitter dispute with the Child Support Agency has been found hanged.
Colleagues discovered Steve Willey, 45, dead at his home after he failed to turn up for duty.

Close friend Jan Kopec, 52, said Mr Willey had told him payments to his ex-wife, by whom he had a ten-year-old son, had trebled to £90 a week since the CSA had become involved.

It is understood that at a divorce hearing last week Mr Willey was ordered to pay a total of £50,000 in maintenance – although it is not known at what rate this is to be paid. Another friend said: "With everything that had gone on with the CSA, the court case was the last straw. He had put his house up for sale to try to pay the money."

Sub-officer Peter Isaacs, Mr Willey's chief on Red Watch at Christchurch, Dorset, said: "He was deeply unhappy about the way the CSA treated him and said they were delving into every aspect of his financial affairs. He felt very aggrieved and was depressed by it. He would say the CSA wanted 11/10ths of everything."

Brian Taylor, of Dorset NACSA, said: "This is a tragic case which shows how desperately needed major changes to the agency are."

A CSA spokesman said: "It is always a matter of great sadness if someone takes their life but we cannot know all the circumstances that may have led to it."
An inquest will be held.

Clive Cass
Evening Argus October 1994

A hard-up father worried about the Child Support Agency was found dead at a Sussex beauty spot, an inquest heard. Clive Cass was found floating in a pool along the Cuckoo Trail, a mile from his terraced house in Harebeating Drive, Horsebridge, near Hailsham.

A post-mortem showed he probably drowned. Mr Cass's brother, Colin, of Howlett Drive, Hailsham, said the unemployed builder was worried about a letter he had received from the Child Support Agency in April.

But at the time of his death on October 25 the agency had dropped the maintenance request and he owed no money. Mr Cass said: "He'd been divorced for 15 years and had a daughter. A few months before he had received a letter from the CSA. He was worried about it. He was also worried about his health and was convinced he was dying. There was nothing wrong with him as far as I knew. He had met a girl and was happy. He had used all his savings and was worried about that."

Coroner David Wadman recorded an open verdict. Yesterday's inquest was the second in Sussex where the CSA has been accused of playing a part in a dads death.

In April, Goolam Hassen, 53, was found dead at his flat at the Goffs, Eastbourne, with a letter from the CSA on the table in front of him. He had taken a lethal cocktail of drink and drugs after reading the demand for £3,000 in back payment, three times more than he actually owed.

After Mr Hassen's death the CSA said it would try harder to make sure it did not send incorrect demands to fathers.

Stuart Holloway
The Independent 25 November 1994

Stuart Holloway, father of a three-year-old boy, was found dead in a fume-filled car shortly after receiving cash demands from the CSA.

Stuart, aged 23 from Sandwell Valley, West Bromwich told his girlfriend, Sarah Horton, that the agency could "stuff the money". He went on a two-day spending spree and then killed himself.

Jason Game
Cambridgeshire Town Crier 17 December 1994

A man found hanging in the Coneygeare area of Eynesbury last month killed himself while suffering from depression. Jason Anthony Game (28) of Philip Garden, Eynesbury, was found hanging from a tree on the morning of Monday, November 21.

An inquest at Huntingdon on Tuesday was told that at the time of his death he was divorcing his wife and had debts to clear.

He was also receiving letters from the Child Support Agency. Mr Game had been married twice before and had three children. His girlfriend, Anita Rendell-Read, said: "He was always kind but in the last few weeks he had been quiet and had been ignoring letters from the CSA. His biggest problem was with his children. He always wanted to do the right thing by them but he was constantly battling with 'red tape'. Why could the CSA not see that?"

She also told the inquest that on the day he died he got up to go to work as usual. However, he did not take his work boots or his bike from the garage. When told of his death, she discovered there was a length of blue nylon rope missing from the garage, which he had used to hang himself.

His body was found by a policeman near to the river bank in Eynesbury. Pc Ian Simmons, based at St Neots, told the inquest: "I saw a body hanging from a tree and there was a blue length of nylon rope around his neck. I searched the area but did not find a suicide note."

Deputy coroner, Dr Colin Latimer, said: "For some period of time Mr Game was under pressure and became withdrawn and depressed. It is quite clear to me that he killed himself while suffering from depression."

A post-mortem found that the cause of death was asphyxia due to strangulation with a ligature.

Garrett Williams
Leicester Mercury March 1995

A father killed himself the day after a flare up with his girlfriend on St Valentine's Day, a Leicester inquest heard. Mr Garrett Williams (37) had been arguing with her over money for their children and matters came to a head when he received a letter from the Child Support Agency.

Mr Williams, of Peter's Road, Leicester, took his own life on February 15 this year by tying electrical cord round his throat. He left two suicide notes and the inquest heard that he had been suffering from depression. The cause of death was given as a ligature round the neck and assistant coroner Mr Michael Charman recorded a verdict of suicide.

Mark Corkish
Scottish Daily Record 17 April 1995

A mother yesterday accused the Child Support Agency of hounding her son to his death.

Mark Corkish, who became a father at 14, was found dead in his flat after taking a lethal cocktail of pills and weedkiller. Just hours earlier, 24-year-old Mark gave his kids Lee, nine, and Cherelle, six, his last six pounds.

He told them: "I want the two of you to have this because where I'm going I won't be needing it."

The children's mum, Wendy Allen, said they used the money to buy her an Easter egg.

Mark's mum, 57-year-old Agnes Corkish, sobbed: "It was a needless death. If they'd never cut his giro. I'd still have my boy today."

Mark, who was found dead in Edinburgh last Wednesday, received £72 a fortnight Income Support but his benefit was cut after he left a training course because he was embarrassed about his dyslexia.

Then the Child Support Agency clawed back a further £10, leaving him just £21.50 a week to live on.

Wendy, of Leith, said: "I never saw any of the money the CSA took from Mark. They didn't need to do it that way, anyway. "Mark always gave the kids what he could, even if it was only 50p."

A spokesman for the CSA said he couldn't comment on individual cases. But he added: "The CSA is always willing to discuss any worries people may have about their case if they contact us. It's a matter of great sadness when someone takes their own life but we can't know all the circumstances which may have led to it."

The CSA have been credited with causing a string of suicides. Nine men have killed themselves since the agency was set up in 1993.

John Rudden
Scottish Daily Record 17 April 1995

... all we know is that, last year, John Rudden, of Rutherglen, threw himself off a bridge over the M74 and that only this month Mark Corkish from Leith in Edinburgh swallowed a cocktail of pills and weedkiller and killed himself. Both were reported to be having severe problems with the Child Support Agency.

Anthony Clemson
Shropshire Star 25 April 1995

The CSA has been blamed by a family for the death of a midlands man. Father-of-two Anthony Clemson of Wolverhampton killed himself because he faced a staggering demand for money from the Child Support Agency. He was found hanging in London the day after receiving a letter ordering him to pay £105 a week maintenance to his estranged wife.

He faced the demand because delays in handling the case had run up arrears of nearly £8,000. Today his mother said she believed the CSA had pushed him too far: "Anthony would be alive today if it hadn't been for them," said 47-year-old Mrs Theresa Clemson of Shelley Road, Fordhouses.

Mr Clemson lived there with his parents after separating from his wife Helen. He saw his daughters Sheryl, six, and Toni, four, at least once a week. "He bought them clothes and things and took them out and into town, and made sure they didn't want for anything," said his mother.

She said the separation was acrimonious and he preferred to buy the girls things rather than pay maintenance through his wife. Mrs Clemson said that her son took home £173 a week from his job and paid her £25 board.

Mr Clemson who was found hanged on April 9, was buried at Bushbury Cemetery on 24 April 1995.
An inquest has been opened, with the cause of death given as hanging. A CSA spokeswoman said the agency never commented on individual cases.

Brian Smith
Today & The Telegraph 13 May 1995

A prison officer killed himself because he could not pay £150 a week to the CSA which ignored letters from his former wife stating categorically she did not need the money.

Brian Smith, 42, the father of three teenage daughters, was found on a settee at his home in Whitchurch, Cardiff, with empty pill bottles strewn on the floor. A note next to his body said: "To whom it may concern, I am just about fed up with being here. I just can't take any more. I just feel so alone and isolated."

His ex-wife, Gaynor, said he had been paying her £33 every week and covering their mortgage before the Child Support Agency became involved. "I didn't want any more money from Brian. We were more than happy with what he had been paying. I even wrote to the CSA telling them I didn't want the money but I heard nothing from them."

Eight months after his death the family received a letter offering to lower the payment.
An inquest heard that Mr Smith was unable to pay his household bills on top of the CSA demands and was left £7 short every week.

His cousin, Howard Cotter, said: "The CSA did have a bearing on his death – even they have admitted that to me. If the CSA hadn't hounded him so much, he would still be alive."

Michael Aston
Daily Express 26 July 1995

A father-of-seven killed himself after getting a bill for more than £10,000 from the Child Support Agency. An inquest heard that Michael Aston, 48 was found dead in his fume-filled car a day after getting the maintenance arrears demand. He had been told to pay £150 a week for three children from a previous marriage. He had previously paid £3.50 a week per child.

But the bill was an interim figure because Mr Aston, of Birmingham, had not properly completed a form stating he was unemployed, the city hearing heard. The arrears could have been written off if he had.

Gardner Clifford Peacock
Basingstoke Gazette 18 August 1995

A Hampshire father gassed himself in his car because he could not cope crippling financial demands from the Child Support Agency, an inquest heard. Gardener Clifford Peacock, aged 34, drove to a secluded beauty spot after receiving a letter from the CSA telling him to increase his maintenance. He connected a hose pipe to the exhaust of his Vauxhall Nova and fed it through a window with the engine still running. Mr Peacock's fiancee, Barbara Williams, said he was having difficulty finding the money to pay his ex-wife, who looked after their children. He took on more and more work in an effort to meet payments. She said: "He was becoming more and more angry about it."

The jury was told that in June this year, Mr Peacock, of Worting, near Basingstoke, packed all his belongings and left the home he shared with Miss Williams. Eight days later he was found dead in his car at Abbotstone Down, Alresford. Mid Hants Coroner Graham Short recorded a verdict of suicide. He said: "The final pressure which caused him to take his life was the maintenance he had to pay and the future must have appeared very bleak."

Michael Horner
Bedfordshire on Sunday 27 August 1995

Demands for cash from the Child Support Agency caused a Clifton (near Bedford) man to commit suicide. Michael Horner had become deeply depressed because he was unable to meet large maintenance payments ordered by the agency for the upkeep of a child from a previous marriage. His decomposed corpse was found in a car at Langford on Monday 21 August. A hose pipe had been attached to the exhaust.

Mr Horner, a caterer, had been missing from his home for two days. He lived with his second wife Pauline and despite making an amicable settlement with his ex-wife in court, the CSA plagued him with demands for vastly increased maintenance payments. Speaking before his funeral his wife said: "The CSA was a big factor in his death. He's dead now and nothing is going to bring him back."

A CSA spokesman said: "The CSA is always willing to discuss any worries people have about their cases if they contact us. It's a matter of great sadness when anybody takes his own life but we can't know all the circumstances which may have led to it. Like any other organisation responsible for enforcing legal or financial responsibilities, the agency sometimes has to enter people's lives with news that might well add to their existing problems. We make every effort to ensure that such legal liabilities are dispatched accurately."

Philip Mitchell
Jonathan Mitchell
Cathryn Mitchell
Jessica Mitchell
Christopher Mitchell
Manchester Evening News, The Sentinel, 30 September - 2 October 1995

The mother of four children who died alongside their father in a fume-filled car said her ex-husband, Philip, had been beset with crippling financial problems.

But Linda Mitchell said he had just received a demand for £2,800 from the Child Support Agency and ordered to pay £51.10 a week maintenance within days.

"He was very quiet and subdued. There was the gradual build-up of debts and the final statement was the last straw," said Mrs Mitchell.

She and the children also faced losing their home at Rudheath, Northwich, Cheshire, because of mortgage arrears.

Friends of Philip said: "Money was the problem and the CSA demand was the final straw.

Philip Mitchell (36) worked as a machine operator for Ilford Films while at night he cleaned on the industrial estate at Middlewich where his fume-filled car was found. He was discovered slumped in the driver's seat and with him were his children, Jonathan, Cathryn, Christopher and Jessica. They were wearing their new school uniforms and toffees bought for them by their father were scattered on the floor. A hose led from the exhaust pipe and the engine was still running.

Philip Mitchell had rented a housing association flatlet to be nearer to his children and had secretly taken on the second job in an attempt to pay off the CSA.

He had divorced his wife after 15 years of marriage but always saw the children regularly and would baby-sit when his ex-wife went out.

"He thought the world of the kids and despite the debts he still treated them the same way – as if money problems were not there," said a tearful Mrs Mitchell. "He had just spent £140 on school uniforms and £100 on shoes. This was his way of saying he thought the world of the kids and loved them."

The four children were buried in the graveyard of St Helen's Church, under a Hawthorn tree yards from their school playing field in Northwich, Cheshire.

Assistant curate the Rev Philip Wain called the tragedy "incomprehensible". He told the 500 mourners that words could not "scratch the surface of the depth of shock we all feel".

Some of the dead children's classmates at Church Walk Primary School were in tears as they left the service. So many have been deeply disturbed that head teacher and Mr Wain toured the school trying to put their minds at rest.
Several pupils have asked teachers: "Could my daddy ever do that to me?"

A CSA spokeswoman said the Agency is always willing to discuss people's worries and that it's a matter of great sadness when anyone takes their own life.

Peter Staffieri
Barrow Evening Mail October 1995

A Barrow policeman killed himself when pressure from the CSA got too much for him, an inquest heard. Coroner Ian Smith recorded a verdict of suicide on Detective Constable Staffieri (38) who was found hanging in the garage of his home.

Mrs Angela Staffieri, the dead man's wife, said he was in constant contact with the CSA and the heavy payments he had to make to support his children "made his life a misery".
Mr and Mrs Staffieri have two children of their own but he was also making payments to the two children from his previous marriage. Mrs Staffieri said her husband received a letter from the CSA saying he could reduce his payments by £40. He took this to mean £40 a week but on the day he died, August 1, he had a second letter which said it was £40 a month.

It was the final straw, Mrs Staffieri said: "He felt he was banging his head against a brick wall. He said he was fed up trying to sort it out. He felt he could not make ends meet because of the amounts the CSA were asking for. When he received the second letter he said there was nothing we could do and he said he was going to move in with a friend and try to support me – he felt that was the only way. I went to settle the children down and when I came downstairs I felt something was wrong. Everything was locked up... that's when I found him."

The coroner said: "He had financial difficulties and felt the CSA were making his life a misery. He didn't feel he was getting anywhere. The second letter caused him great distress and was the final straw. It's clear beyond any doubt that he intended to take his own life."

Joshua Skerton
Plymouth Evening Herald, 24 November 1995

A distraught Plymouth father who killed one son and tried to kill the other in a bungled suicide attempt was jailed for five years at Plymouth Crown Court on 21 November 1994 after admitting the manslaughter of two-year-old Joshua and the grievous bodily harm of Samuel aged four.
The Court heard that little Joshua died after his father, Wayne Skerton, drove him and Sam to Dartmoor on March 23, attached a hose pipe to the exhaust and fed it into his Ford Sierra car.

Skerton had planned that all three would die together but the engine overheated and stalled. All three were given specialist treatment at Fort Bovisland Diving Diseases Research Centre but Joshua suffered brain damage and died a few days later.

Mrs Skerton said she could not come to terms with the fact that the man she had loved since she was 14 could have harmed their two sons. "I know he loved them and they loved their daddy too. But you don't do this to people you love, no matter how bad you are feeling," she said. Wayne split with his wife and left the family home in Brixton earlier in the year. But he couldn't come to terms with it and was under pressure from the CSA.

Detective Inspector Stuart Newberry said the judge had had a difficult job to decide on the right sentence.

Graham Clay
Daily Express 7 December 1995

A stately home's curator killed himself after the Child Support Agency more than doubled his maintenance payments, his family said yesterday.

Police called to Newstead Abbey, near Nottingham, found Graham Clay, 31, hanging from a staircase, surrounded by papers the family said were documents and letters about payments ordered by the government body.

The day before he died, Mr Clay had received a letter from the agency asking for payments to his ex-wife and two children of £252 a month out of £500 income after tax. He had previously agreed on £100 a month with his former wife, Wendy. The couple were married 12 years ago and the divorce was finalised two months ago.

The body was found on Saturday in the entrance hall of the home of Lord Byron, where Mr Clay had been head guide. According to relatives he left a note blaming the agency.

After the £252 assessment in August, he had visited his ex-wife and children and, according to a family friend, had given no indication that he was planning suicide. His former wife had apparently offered to return much of the extra maintenance because she thought the award unfair.

Mr Clay had been renting a room in Mapperley, Nottingham, from his aunt, Josie Clay, 55, who said yesterday: "He was devastated... It left him no money to start the new life he had been longing for or to buy Christmas presents for his children."

Last week an inquest in Boston, Lincolnshire, heard how Brian Gorton, 42, a draughtsman hanged himself after the CSA doubled his maintenance payments to £200 a month when his former wife separated from a second husband.

David Harmsworth
Sussex Evening Argus 21/22 December 1995

A father of four killed himself while under pressure from the controversial Child Support Agency, an inquest heard. David Harmsworth aged 45, of Coldean, Brighton, was found dead on November 20. He was discovered in his van parked at the Braypool sports ground in Patcham, by a man taking his dog for a walk. A hose was taped from the exhaust. A postmortem revealed that he died from carbon monoxide poisoning.

Mr Harmsworth, a plumber and former driving instructor, had been suffering from depression. The inquest heard that he left letters that made it clear he intended to take his own life. His sister, Katerina Steele, from Lancing, told the Brighton hearing he had financial problems and owed money to the CSA for two children he no longer saw.

She said: "He had the CSA after him for money. Last December he said he owed £2,000. He was not allowed to see his two youngest children, which upset him dreadfully."

His former fiancé, Tracy Simmons, from Portslade, said he had been suffering depression for some time. She said: "The Child Support Agency was asking for an unfair amount of money which he did not have. The assessment was unfair because it did not leave him enough to live on."

East Sussex coroner, Dr Donald Gooding, who recorded a verdict of suicide, told the hearing he had contacted the CSA but the Agency had declined to comment on the case as the information was covered by the Data Protection Act. He said: "This is a sad story. He clearly had a number of problems, both financial and domestic. I have no evidence the CSA assessment was unreasonable."

A spokesperson from the Brighton and Worthing branch of NACSA said: "This latest tragedy brings the total to 36 wasted lives in the last two years. It cannot keep going on like this. People are under intolerable stress. The pressure really does drag you down. These deaths are not just isolated incidents. The CSA has been the main factor in most of these deaths."

A spokesman for the Agency said: "The reasons why people choose to commit suicide are many and complicated. Anybody who has problems with payments should talk to the Agency which is always willing to try to come to some sort of arrangement."

Alex Nicholson
Sussex Evening Argus 21/22 December 1995

Former village bobby, Alex Nicholson aged 36, who once attacked the CSA because of the financial pressure it was placing him under, was found dead last month. Mr Nicholson was discovered in Germany after going missing from his home in Cuckfield, near Haywards Heath.

Tony Cummings
Runcorn Weekly News March 1996

A soldier being pursued by the Child Support Agency was found hanging in his bedroom, an inquest at Warrington heard.

Kingsman Tony Cummings had been contacted by the CSA after a woman claimed he was the father of her child, the inquest was told. Mr Cummings, aged 22, of Greebridge Road, Runcorn, was found by his mother hanging from a hook in his bedroom while on leave.

The inquest heard that Mr Cummings had been seeing a girl for two years and was very happy. But then he had a 'one night stand' with another woman.

He joined the army soon after and split up with his girlfriend. But the other woman then began to contact him claiming he was the father of her child.

He attended an interview with the CSA with his father and afterwards seemed to be very depressed and unhappy.

While on leave he had seemed fairly cheerful and had been out drinking with his father. He returned home and went upstairs. A short time later his mother went up to turn his stereo off and found him hanging from a metal hook in the ceiling with pictures and old letters from his girlfriend.

A fellow soldier, Stephen Birchall, said: "Tony was worried about the amount of money he would have to pay to the CSA."

Alan Grantham
Rochdale Express 7 June 1996

A father-of-two who was found dead in a fume filled car outside his Heywood girlfriend's home was being pursued by the Child Support Agency. Police discovered several payment demands from the CSA strewn about the Ford Orion car in which Alan Grantham was found slumped. A pipe had been fixed from the inside to the exhaust.

Before he died Mr Grantham, aged 39, had left a lengthy message on his girlfriend's answerphone. Police are now examining both the papers and the message.

At an inquest in Rochdale this week deputy coroner Dennis Everett did not disclose the contents of the tape. But he added: "Papers from the CSA for monies outstanding were found in the car."

Policewoman Dorothy Orr said she found the vehicle parked near a school with its engine running around 1:20 am on Monday, 6 May, in Magdala Street, Heywood. There were four people in the middle of the road near the car when she arrived.

In a statement she said: "A piece of black plastic piping had been found running from the exhaust into the car. There was also smoke billowing out of the car's open doors. The piping lay in the road by the time I arrived."

WPc Orr saw Mr Grantham in the driver's seat, which was reclined. His eyes were closed. She called an ambulance and checked Mr Grantham for a pulse, but found none. Police later called at the terraced home of Miss Lyndsey Scholes, the dead man's girlfriend. She gave the police a tape from her telephone answering machine.

The Network Against the Child Support Act has collected a dossier of over a dozen men who they claim have committed suicide because of cash demands from the CSA.

Nigel Ryan
South Wales Argus 28 June 1996

The CSA came under fire from Gwent coroner Mr David Bowen yesterday, for causing the death of a young father from Chepstow, whose body was found in his fume-filled car. He said notes left by Nigel Ryan, of Wyedean, made it clear that letters from the CSA and a court appearance due the following week, were the triggers for his actions.

He went on: "For some months prior to his death he had needed psychiatric help, which he refused. That mental condition was in no small part brought about by demands from the CSA.

He recorded a verdict at the Abergavenny inquest that 36-year-old Mr Ryan, who had married just twelve months earlier, had killed himself while the balance of his mind was disturbed.

At the inquest, Mrs Sandra Ryan said her husband, who worked as a steelworker, had needed psychiatric help for six months before his death because he felt everyone was against him and he dreaded going to work.

"I tried to persuade him to go to the doctor but he refused and asked me to go for him and get a sick note, so he did not have to go to work," she said.

"He had received a letter from the CSA asking him to appear in court, and then another letter adjourned the hearing until the Thursday after his death. I was concerned about the effect this appearance might have on him. It had been playing on his mind for some time."

She said he left for work on April 19 but she received a phone call from his colleagues later that day to say he had not turned up for work.

Mr Bowen said Ryan's body was found in his fume filled car in Wentwood Forest the following morning and he had letters in the vehicle relating to the CSA. After the inquest, Krys Simmonds, press officer for the CSA, said the agency was not asked to give evidence at the inquest but was fully prepared to do so and believed their evidence may have helped.

"The agency sometimes enters people's lives with news that may add to their existing problems. It is a matter of great sadness when anyone takes their own life but we cannot know all the circumstances which may have led to it."

Robert McWhirter
Unknown

Robert McWhirter from Rutherglen killed himself at the end of 1995. He had been in regular contact with the CSA in Falkirk and in the latter days had pleaded with them to allow him time to get his financial affairs in order. However, the officer he spoke to refused to give him any leeway. McWhirter told him bluntly he couldn't go on like this and that if the CSA wouldn't stop pressuring him he'd commit suicide.

The CSA officer in Falkirk retorted: "Be sure to tell us first who your executors are." A few days later he was dead.

At the time of the incident the CSA officer concerned was on his second warning for similar behaviour of this kind. He still works at Falkirk CSAC.

Leslie Pearson
Citizen on Sunday April 1997

Visitors to Furzton Lake failed to spot a man hanging in a tree until mid-afternoon, where he had been since the early hours of the morning. Even police who had visited the lake's car park earlier in the day to investigate a car with the keys let in the ignition – later discovering it was the dead man's car – failed to spot him.

An inquest on Thursday heard 39-year-old Leslie Pearson of Bletchley seemed to have planned the hanging on March 1 this year, telling his stepdaughter and her young children the night before it will all be over in seven hours. But she hadn't taken him seriously, even though he had mentioned he would use the tow rope from the car because he was so drunk and could hardly stand up.

Mr Pearson a printer's assistant who had left his wife Sue six weeks earlier, had given up his job the day before. Mrs Pearson told Milton Keynes Coroner Rodney Corner she believed her husband of seven years would come back to her eventually.

The inquest heard Mr Pearson had bank debts of more than £1,000 and he owed money to the Child Support Agency for payments to two teenage children from a former relationship.

William Pigg
Daily Express 13 May 1997

A father stabbed to death his former wife's husband in a frenzied attack after the Child Support Agency seized over half his wages, the Old Bailey heard on Monday. John Reid, 54, confronted William Pigg on the doorstep of his home hours after receiving a demand for £206 a month maintenance from his gross salary of £560.

Orlando Pownall, prosecuting, said Reid pulled an eight inch knife and stabbed Mr Pigg 10 times in the head, arm and body screaming: "Die you bastard, die". Mr Pigg, 30, died shortly afterwards. In 1996, the CSA had asked Reid for £13 a week in maintenance for his 13-year-old daughter. Reid, of Hampton, Middlesex, who denies murder, then telephoned the CSA and said: "This situation could have a very, very tragic outcome."

He quit his £23,000 a year job as a Heathrow Airport supervisor and later took a part-time job and sold his home for £46,000 giving his former wife half. He was £1,000 in arrears with maintenance, and had declared himself bankrupt, when he learnt that a deduction of £206 was being made from his wages. When he saw it he told a colleague. "I do not believe this – they are robbing me."

Reid later told police: "The CSA said my payments had increased because I was homeless. I went to talk to Mr Pigg to see if he would give me some money. He started shouting and saying terrible things about my marriage. He hit me a glancing blow. I hoped that if I poked him he would stop."

Evening Standard 20 may 1997

A father, who said he was driven to kill by the CSA when they began taking almost half his wages, was found not guilty of murder today. John Reid, 54, was convicted of manslaughter on the grounds of provocation and jailed for seven years for killing his former wife's new husband.

The court was told that Mr Pigg had badgered the CSA to increase payments for his 13-year-old daughter Stephanie. The agency, learning Reid was homeless, reasoned he would have more money available to pay his ex-wife.

David Piggott
Unknown, July 1997

A mother has blamed the CSA for her son's suicide and is calling on the Government to have the organisation abolished. Junette Piggott's son David, 33, of Wrexham, took an overdose after falling £6,000 in arrears while waiting for the CSA to deal with his case.

"They killed him as surely as if they had put a shotgun to his head and pulled the trigger," she said as she left an inquest on Wednesday. Wiping away tears, Mrs Piggott said officials had not listened to repeated pleas for help.

The Wrexham hearing was told that before the CSA become involved, the conscientious welder, who liked to pay up on the dot, made regular payments under a court order for his ex-girlfriends eight-year-old daughter. But his income dropped from £1,600 a month to £1,100 and he telephoned and wrote to the CSA asking for new assessment to match his reduced earnings. He said the delay was pushing him into debt.

Producing a file of letters he had written, his new partner Lynne Hughes said he was worried about arrears. Then he was sent a £6,000 bill which he could not pay. "He was willing to pay," she said, "but when that huge bill came he was devastated." By reading an agency booklet he became convinced he had only to pay arrears for six months but the words were misleading and, in fact, he had to meet payments for 18 months.

He was so worried he could not sleep at night and he saw his doctor. On November 24 he went missing after being out with a friend for a drink and his body was found three days later in woods outside the town.

Leslie Moorcroft, senior manager of the CSA's Birkenhead office, said pressure of work had prevented staff dealing with MR Piggott's assessment more quickly or writing to him to explain the delay. "It is regrettable," he said, and agreed with North-East Wales Coroner John Hughes that the leaflet was poorly worded and capable of giving the wrong impression that only six months arrears must be paid.

Recording a verdict of suicide the Coroner said: "The consequence of your failure to explain his arrears is that he has taken his own life. You should use words as clear as crystal."

He went on: "I think it is a matter of public knowledge that there have been other incidents where persons have found themselves under pressure to pay through the CSA and there have been previous inquests involving the agency."

CSA spokeswoman Kris Symmonds said for the CSA that all literature was under review. "We shall consider the coroner's recommendations as soon as possible," she said.

Aubrey Scott
Reading Chronicle 5 June 1998

A Reading man who told friends the Child Support Agency was "after him" died after hurling himself from a bridge onto the M4 motorway an inquest heard this week.
Friend and workmate Gary Hart said Mr Scott phoned him the previous Sunday saying he had 'messed up' and was going to spend his last money on a beer.

Mr Hart found out from BT that he had called from a payphone in Berkeley Avenue and drove there, finding him sitting on the railway bridge with his legs dangling over the IDR.

He talked Mr Scott down and took him to his mother's house, and he added: "He didn't say much, but he said the CSA was after him and that he wanted to get back with his wife."
At 10.30 am the following Saturday, March 28, Whitley mechanic Steven Raymond saw Mr Scott standing on the bridge over the M4 on the Shinfield Road, near the Black Boy pub.

Mr Raymond said: "As I got by the side of him he bent his legs and jumped."

He died from head and neck injuries and, recording a suicide verdict, Reading coroner Dr Joe Pim said: "We've heard he was in a state over finances and accommodation and there had been a similar episode a week earlier.

"I have no doubt that Aubrey did this on purpose."

Andrew Pinch
Lancashire Evening Telegraph 27 August 1998

A man involved in a long-running dispute with the Child Support Agency hanged himself after a night out.

An inquest into the death of Andrew Pinch, 25, of Whalley Road, Clitheroe, heard that on the day of his death £203 had been deducted from his pay of £293.

Flat mate Steven Cudworth, now of Riverside, Clitheroe, had discovered the body hanging by a plastic coated bicycle padlock chain from a bannister.

He had been out with Andrew and other friends at a 21st birthday party. Andrew had left before them after a minor altercation with another friend, Gareth Wareing, of Moorland Crescent, Clitheroe.

In a statement read to the inquest Mr Wareing said Andrew had seemed a bit down.

"He asked me if I believed in life after death and said he would prove it to everyone that there was life after death," said Mr Wareing.

Justin Townson, a colleague at Ultraframe, in Clitheroe, said Andrew was concerned about the amount of money the Child Support Agency was taking from his wage and about the fact that he was not seeing a lot of his three year old son.

"We were sitting in his front room and he turned round and said "I should kill myself" said Mr Townson.

The inquest heard that Andrew had taken three months unpaid leave from work and gone to visit friends in Australia. When he returned in May, there were arrears in his child support payments. His supervisor at work, Michael Stewart, said that after his return Andrew had struggled to come to terms with new working methods and his problems had eventually led to disciplinary procedure.

"He had this problem with the Child Support Agency and we had talked about the shares he would be able to cash in October," said Mr Stewart.

Coroner Andre Rebello read a case history provided by the Child Support Agency which suggested that Andrew had not responded when case review forms were issued.

On May 26, ten days before he died, the Citizens' Advice Bureau had contacted the agency on his behalf and said that he had made a lump sum payment to his child's mother before he went to Australia.

The agency said he should put the facts in writing but they never received anything. Mr Rebello recorded a verdict that Andrew killed himself.

Gary Ashton
Sheffield Star 22 October 1998

A divorced father-of-two found dead in his fume filled car blamed his own death on the Child Support Agency.

Caretaker Gary Ashton, 33, drove his Ford Escort into a garage, pulled down the roller door, attached a hose to the exhaust pipe, fed it through the car window then locked himself inside and started the engine.

His body was found next day by a close friend concerned that he had not been seen at his flat in Harold Lambert Court, Hyde Park.

Police officers who attended the scene found an envelope addressed to his father and sisters on the dashboard. In it was a note in which Gary begged his family not to blame girlfriend Rachael Smith for his death.

She left him just weeks before resentful that he had to pay almost £300 a month to his ex-wife towards the upkeep of his children Nathan, eight, and Danika, seven, according to Sheffield coroner Chris Dorries.

At an inquest into the tragedy details of the apparent suicide note were read out. The letter said: "The CSA is killing me, don't blame Rachael. It's not down to her."

The Star understands that Gary's former wife Carol wrote to the agency before his death urging them to cut the amount he had to pay.

"Gary was a good dad; he loved the kids and saw them most weekends. He gave them everything he could afford, but the CSA were asking him to pay too much and it was getting him down," said Carol.

His father, Jack Ashton, of Ravenscroft Avenue, Stradbroke, has also written to the agency blaming them for Gary's death. Mr Ashton said, "I am convinced that the way they hounded him led him to what he did.

"I wrote to tell them that this time they had struck gold - but they haven't even had the decency to reply to me."
The inquest into Gary's death will resume next week. The CSA has declined to comment until Mr Dorries records his verdict.

Sheffield Star 29 October 1998

Child Support Agency bosses have ordered an investigation after a father-of-two killed himself - and blamed his death on them. Officials from the controversial agency have written to the family of Gary Ashton promising to launch an investigation into his death. But Gary's father, Jack, said nothing could make up for the loss of his son.

"They're just fobbing us off," he said. "I know they're to blame and nothing they say will make up for that."

Recording a verdict that Mr Ashton took his own life Coroner Chris Dorries said a number of factors may have been responsible. He said: "It is quite apparent that Mr Ashton had a number of problems facing him. In all respects this was a particularly sad case."

A spokesman from the CSA declined to comment on any enquiry.

Mark Harrison
Yorkshire Evening Press 28 August 1998

A father committed suicide after receiving a £300 a month demand from the Child Support Agency, an inquest was told. Mark John Harrison, a 33-year-old clerical officer with BT, could not afford the money because he was already paying the mortgage and all the bills for his former wife and their child, said his father, John Harrison, in a statement at the hearing at Scarborough.

Mr Harrison, of Thomas Street, Barlby Road, Selby, had been found dead in his fume-filled car at a quarry at Flixton near Scarborough after several previous suicide attempts, the inquest heard.

His wife Lesley said in a statement that he had been depressed about money. On one occasion she found him hanging from the attic with a flex around his neck, and he had tried to kill himself by fixing a hose to his car exhaust and taking an overdose.

When she left him, taking their baby with her, he had told her he would take his life. "I told him the threat would not make me return," she said.

Joanne Dennis, who worked with Mr Harrison at BT, said they had started a relationship and she became pregnant. They quarrelled and the CSA "took him to the cleaners financially" over his marriage.

The North Yorkshire East Coroner, Michael Oakley, recorded a verdict that he took his own life.

John Johnson
Nottingham Evening Post 10 February 1999

A father killed himself after blaming the Child Support Agency for leaving him penniless.

John Johnson, 40, sent a suicide note to the agency saying he had "decided to die" because he could not afford to live. He electrocuted himself at his Hucknall flat.

Mr Johnson's parents - Henry and Mary - today criticised the agency and said it had driven their son to suicide. Mrs Johnson, 60, said: "He felt he could not go on any longer because the CSA was taking so much money.

"What they were doing was wrong.He just wanted to sort out sensible payments and now he is dead."

Notts coroner Dr Nigel Chapman recorded a verdict of suicide at a Nottingham inquest. He said Mr Johnson, of St James Court, had sent several notes, including the one to the CSA.

In a note found on his bed, he wrote: "Life is not worth living with the CSA taking so much money." Police found MR Johnson's body on February 1 after being contacted by the CSA.

The inquest heard he was divorced in October and was paying £62 a week maintenance for his 11-year-old son. Mrs Johnson, from Lincolnshire, told the hearing her son had tried to take his life before, when he came depressed after his marriage ended.

He had got his life back in order, however, and was doing well until the CSA started demanding payments.
"It left him with £85 a week to pay his bills rent and living expenses," she said.

"He had no money but was such a proud man he would not ask us for help."

CSA spokesman Ian Cuddy daid the agency would not take more than 30 per cent of someone's income.

He added: "It is tragic when someone takes their own life. The CSA touches people's lives when they are already under great stress but we are always willing to discuss individual problems."

Mr Johnson's MP, Paddy Tipping, today renewed calls for changes in the CSA, branding it a shambles.

The Guardian 11 February 1999

A father sent a note to the Child Support Agency before electrocuting himself at his flat, an inquest in Nottingham was told yesterday. John Johnson, aged 40, of Hucknall in Nottinghamshire, was found dead on February 1 after the agency contacted police. The note read: "I will not work again because you will only steal 50 per cent of my earnings. I will not live with what I have left and have decided to die."

A spokesman for the CSA said it recognised people became involved with it when they were already under great stress, and was always willing to discuss individual problems. Roslyn Johnson, the deceased's former wife, and their children Gemma, aged 18, and Nathan, aged 11, were not at their Hucknall home yesterday.

His mother, Mary Johnson, aged 60, of Sleaford in Lincolnshire, said the agency was asking him for more than £60 a week, leaving him with £80 to live on. Verdict: Suicide.

Eastern Daily Press 11 February 1999

A 40-year-old father sent a suicide note to the Child Support Agency before electrocuting himself.

John Johnson, of Hucknall, Nottinghamshire, was found dead on February 1 after the CSA contacted police to say they had received the note.

An inquest heard that Mr Johnson had sent several notes including the one to the CSA. It read: "I will not work again because you will only steal 50 per cent of my earnings. I will not live with what I have left and have decided to die." Another note found at his home read: "Life is not worth living with the CSA taking so much money."

His mother Mary Johnson, 60, of Sleaford, Linconshire, said: "He was very upset when his marriage broke up, but managed to get over that. Then the CSA were asking for more than £60 a week and that left him with about £80 to live on."

Ian Cuddy, spokesman for the CSA, said: "It is tragic when someone takes their own life.

"The CSA touches people's lives when they are under great stress, but we are always willing to discuss individual problems."

Notts coroner Dr Nigel Chapman recorded a verdict of suicide. Mr Johnson's ex-wife Roslyn and children Gemma, 18 and Nathan, 11, were not at home yesterday.

Unknown Publication 11 February 1999

The parents of a man who committed suicide today criticised the Child Support Agency, saying it had driven him to desperation.

John Johnson (40) electrocuted himself in his flat after sending a note to the CSA saying he had decided to die because he could no longer afford to live.

His parents Henry (67) and Mary Johnson (60) from Heckinton, near Sleaford today spoke of their anger at his death.

Mrs Johnson said: "He felt he couldn't go on any longer because the CSA was taking so much money. What they were doing was wrong. He just wanted to sort out sensible payments and now he is dead."

In the note he sent to the CSA, John Johnson said: "I will not work again because you will only steal 50 per cent of my earnings. I will not live with what I have left and have decided to die."

Police found Mr Johnson's body in his Nottingham flat on February 1 after being contacted by the CSA who had received his suicide note. He was found wired up to the mains. Coroner Dr Nigel Chapman recorded a verdict of suicide at an inquest yesterday.

The inquest heard that Mr Johnson was divorced in October and was paying £62 a week for maintenance for his 11-year-old son.

His mother Mary told the inquest that her son had attempted to take his life after his marriage broke down, but in the months before his death he had got his life back in order until the demands came through from the CSA.

He was a quality control inspector with Bell's Fruits in Nottingham where he was picking up £147 per week. His mother said he had to pay £62 to the CSA, £40 for the car, £32 for rent and £10 on council tax which left him with £3 a week for anything else. His mother was helping him out with £50 per fortnight.

She said: "The CSA got in touch with him almost immediately after the divorce. I blame the CSA for my son's death. We are absolutely devastated. Nobody should have to go through what we went through."

A CSA spokesman said the agency would not take more than 40 percent of an individual's income.

"It is tragic when someone takes their own life. The CSA touches people's lives when they are already under great stress, but we are always willing to discuss problems," he said.

Hucknall & Bulwell Dispatch 12 February 1999

Left with only £3 to live on, a Hucknall man wrote a note that said: "I have decided to die"

The mother of a Hucknall man who killed himself claims the CSA made life impossible for him. John Johnson (40) died from electrocution at his flat in St James's Court, as was exclusively reported in last week's Dispatch.

He was divorced last October and was paying £62 a week maintenance for his 11-year-old son. His mother, Mary Johnson (60), told a Nottingham Inquest: "The CSA was taking so much of his money that he felt he could not go on any longer."

Mrs Johnson of Sleaford, Lincolnshire, said her son had tried to take his life previously when he became depressed after his marriage ended, but he had started to get back on his feet and was doing well until the CSA started demanding payments from him.

It meant he had only £85 a week to pay his rent and other living expenses, leaving him with just £3. "I would like to know how anybody could live on that," said Mrs Johnson. Mr Johnson sent a note to the CSA saying he would never work again. He claimed the CSA would 'steal' 50 per cent of his wages and he would not be able to live with what was left, so he had 'decided to die'.

Pc Michael Topham told the inquest he went to Mr Johnson's home at 2.45 pm on Monday February 1 after the CSA contacted the police about the note. He forced the door and the flat was in complete darkness. He found the body of MR Johnson, who had wired himself up to an electricity mains socket.

One of several notes left by Mr Johnson read: "Life is not worth living with the CSA taking so much money." Recording a suicide verdict, Nottinghamshire Coroner Dr Nigel Chapman said: "I am not going to get involved with outside agencies. But I am satisfied that John has done an act to take his own life."

MP blasts "shambles" that leads to distress. Hucknall's Labour MP, Paddy Tipping, is fighting for changes in the CSA to avoid another tragedy like the death of John Johnson.

Mr Tipping said: "I did not know Mr Johnson but people complain to me about the CSA at all my surgeries. It is a shambles and I have difficulty getting information out of them. Many people suffer real distress as the result of the agency" demands. In Mr Johnson" case, the distress led to his very tragic death."

Mr Tipping said he had spoken separately to the chief executive of the CSA and the junior minister in the department of social security, Baroness Hollis.

"I am confident of new legislation, hopefully in the next parliamentary session, to change the CSA," said Mr Tipping.

"People are being treated very poorly and are very often given wrong answers. I am very sad at what has happened in Mr Johnson's case but it makes me even more determined to get the CSA changed."

Robert Hendry
Lincolshire Echo 1 March 1999

A distraught mother whose son took his own life after a struggle to pay CSA demands is calling for a better deal for dads.

Robert Hendry killed himself because he was unable to cope with paternity payments to children from a previous marriage.

Today, his devastated mum, Amelia Marris, who lives just outside Lincoln, said in his darkest hours no-one could have known what he was going through. "He was in hell," she said.

"There was nobody he could turn to who could understand. I think there should be a support group for men in this situation, someone to turn to for advice."

An inquest heard how Mr Hendry had also been struggling with a relationship since his divorce and couldn't find work. The 32-year-old telephone engineer died of carbon monoxide poisoning last November after driving to a secluded spot in Dunholme, near Lincoln, to take his own life.

A statement by Mrs Marris was read by coroner Roger Atkinson. It asked how many more of Britain's sons would be lost to suicide and called for support to men struggling with depression and CSA demands.

"Robert was always happy to provide for his son and daughter," said Mrs Marris. "He would send them money and parcels of clothes. He was a hard working father and when he lost his job, too proud to sign on the dole."

Mrs Marris said she would be pleased to hear from anyone who would be prepared to lend advice to struggling fathers in similar situations. Robert wouldn't want anyone to go through what he went through, and neither would I," she said.

Lloyd Mather
The Mirror 30 April 1999

A father killed himself after he was wrongly told he'd have to pay more to the CSA, an inquest heard yesterday.
Lloyd Mather, 39, gassed himself in his car.

But ten days after his death a letter to him from the CSA revealed that a mistake had been made. He had actually been overcharged by £700.

The father of two, an engineer, had been very worried about money in the months leading up to his death, the inquest at Winchester heard.

"He said he was having a problem financially with the amount of money the CSA were taking", his father Roy Mather said.

"The CSA changed the amount Lloyd was having to pay at the end of last year and it was upped. After his death his employer received a letter from the CSA saying they had made a mistake to the tune of £700".

Lloyd from Andover, Hants, was found dead in his Mini on the edge of farmland at nearby Tangley by a motorist.

His father added that Lloyd split from his partner ten years ago and she lived in Great Yarmouth with their children.

A former heroin addict Lloyd had become a volunteer worker at a drugs advisory service in Andover. Friend Margaret Cuniffe, the service co-ordinator, said she became worried about him.

"When he became a volunteer he said he had been clean for three years and the problem was behind him." But she said she went to see him in January and knew he must be taking drugs again.

"He was very worried about having to pay more money to the CSA," she said. "He was working but his hours had been cut down."

Mid Hants coroner Grahame Short said: "I don't think we will ever know for sure why he took his own life.

"I think it was a combination of his inability to break his drug habit, the financial pressures he found mounting against him and in particular the problems with the CSA."

Verdict: suicide.

Anthony Tipper
Derbyshire Evening Telegraph 24 August 1999

Mum tells of son's worries over CSA.

The mother of a man who was found dead in a fume-filled car has told how her son was finding it a struggle to cope with maintenance payments demanded by the Child Support Agency.

Forklift driver Anthony Tipper (33) was found dead in his car which was parked in Green Lane at Ellastone.

A post mortem investigation showed Mr Tipper, who lived with his parents, John and Shirley Tipper, in Elm View, Denstone, had died of carbon monoxide poisoning.

Mrs Tipper (59) said: "He was paying maintenance for his six-year-old child. He wasn't arguing about paying, but it was such a big amount out of his wages." Mr Tipper worked for Elkes Biscuits in Uttoxeter and had taken on a weekend job to make ends meet.He died on August 14. A note by him said: "Don't blame anybody. Don't be sad, I'm not."

A CSA spokeswoman said: "We do feel sad when people take their lives, but we cannot comment on any individual cases."

An inquest into Mr Tipper's death was opened and adjourned until a date to be fixed.

Alan Jones
Alan Jones' uncle, Roy Griffiths of Newstead

A father worried about the Child Support Agency arranged his own funeral before taking his life in his bedsit.

Alan Jones whose wife had been contacted by the CSA was found dead in bed after not being seen for nine days. The Coroner, John Wain, said: "...I realise that he was very conscious of the CSA and I feel that his own thoughts about the matter ...played a substantial part in (his) intention to take his own life."

Mr Jones, aged 44 and a former British Rail worker from Fenton in Staffordshire, split from his wife in 1985 but had remained close to her and their son; he continued to pay maintenance and provide extras for the family, visiting most days.

However, he became "very concerned and furious" when the CSA became involved. In particular he became worried about the situation concerning his first wife and her daughter. Alan's uncle, anti CSA campaigner Roy Griffiths of Newstead, confirmed that Alan had arranged his own funeral and he also found a bundle of CSA cuttings and a suicide note whilst clearing his nephew's flat after his death. It read:
"The CSA. With reference to the above, which was brought in through Parliament last year (all parties). I enclose paper cuttings which apply also to myself and no doubt many others. There have been deaths due to this and I can tell you now my name will at some time be another."

Roy said: "The CSA drove Alan to breaking point."

Trevor Lane
Milton Keynes Citizen

When a 24-year-old man learned that his ex-girlfriend had changed the name of his 18-month-old son, it drove him over the edge.

Trevor Lane who lived at Buckingham Square, Central Milton Keynes found out via a letter he received from the CSA that Tracey Corbin from Leighton Buzzard had changed his son Joshua's surname from Lane to Corbin. That night Mr Lane, a lorry driver, killed himself. His body was found in a fume filled car at Willen Lake; the engine was running and a vacuum cleaner hose pipe was attached to the exhaust. Recording a verdict that Mr Lane had killed himself the Coroner said: "I think he decided he couldn't take any more."

Stephen Paul Patience
Grimsby Evening Telegraph (Town & County)

A Grimsby man who had mounting cash worries after being tracked down by the CSA was found hanged in his home. An inquest heard how Stephen Paul Patience (24), of the Cloisters, was discovered by his mother Ann. He was sitting on a dining chair in his hallway with a black flex around his neck.

A post-mortem revealed Mr Patience had 150g of alcohol in his body per 100ml of blood.

Grimsby deputy coroner David Overton recorded a verdict of suicide. The inquest heard Mr Patience was contacted by the CSA at the beginning of 1997 about a child he had fathered. At the time, Mr Patience, who worked as a deck hand, was married and had a two-year-old son.

His mother told the inquest, held at Cleethorpes Town Hall: "This led ultimately to the CSA claiming a large sum of money from Paul. We were aware that this was something which gave great concern to Paul and imposed a great strain on his finances."

On occasions, Mr Patience's parents helped him out financially. "He was so concerned he even wrote to his MP, Austin Mitchell," Mrs Patience told the court.

Last November, the financial problems led Mr Patience's wife to move out, taking their son with her. Mr Patience was prescribed prothiaden for depression by his doctor. A month later, Mr Patience called his mother to his home where he showed her numerous suicide notes he had written. It was two months after that that Mrs Patience discovered her son's body in his hallway. She had gone round to his house after her phone calls were unanswered.

Mr Patience had left three suicide notes – one for his parents and sister, one for his wife and one for his son.

John Leach, a personal friend of the victim writes: (Stephen) Paul was a work colleague of mine who is sadly missed by all of us. This is further proof if needed that, contrary to what the CSA would like everyone to believe, they do ruin people's lives and ultimately cause death.

CSA demands 'drove father to kill himself'
August 2000

THE fiancée of a British Transport policeman who gassed himself in his car has blamed the Child Support Agency for driving him to suicide. Lana Matthews said yesterday that Terry Brett, who had two teenage children, killed himself because of the "impossible" demands made of him by the agency.

Mr Brett, 47, from Murrow Banks, Cambridgeshire, was asked to pay £1,217 a month from his salary of £1,798 towards the maintenance of his children.

He told friends that the money he was left with to support himself was not sufficient to allow him to buy birthday presents for his children.
Mr Brett's suicide brings to 55 the number of deaths linked to the CSA.

The agency has admitted the possibility of potential connections with two deaths. The campaign group NACSA (National Association for Child Support Action) has documented 42 suicides and eight murders that it believes can be laid at the agency's door.

An inquest was told that Mr Brett gassed himself in a car in the garage of his home on January 31. He had attempted to take his life twice before. Ms Matthews, 44, told the inquest in Wisbech, Cambridgeshire, that she woke to hear the car engine running inside the garage. Police officers dragged Mr Brett from the car but they were too late. A verdict of suicide was recorded.

Ms Matthews said later that Mr Brett had been forced to rely on her for financial assistance to pay his mortgage and run his car, a situation that he had difficulty coping with. "He was happy to support his children but the amount the CSA asked for was just impossible for him," she said.

A spokeswoman for the CSA acknowledged that it had been blamed for suicides before but said that she could not comment on specific cases.

Child Support Cases that Set Legal Precedence (Case Law)

In re Fulton, No. 2005-591 (New Hampshire Supreme Court, October 31, 2006): As a matter of statutory interpretation, gifts are not income for purposes of child support. The court may, however, consider gifts as a deviation factor when setting support as part of the overall financial status of the parties.

Lozner v. Lozner (New Jersey Superior Court, Appellate Division, October 30, 2006): When determining if ex-husband's substantial student loan debt warranted alteration of a guidelines-based child support award, trial court should consider whether ex-husband's goals could have been achieved without incurring such overwhelming debt, whether there was a reason ex-husband worked toward his undergraduate and graduate degrees for eleven consecutive years without obtaining a job in between, and whether ex-husband could have gone part time to law school or attended a less expensive school. If a credit card is used to purchase books or pay tuition, this constitutes an educational expense and can be substantially similar to debt incurred through student loans, and substantial student loan debt can constitute a factor to be considered in determining whether alteration of a guidelines-based child support award is warranted; however, credit card debt acquired by a parent to maintain a comfortable life style while attending school is not the substantial equivalent of student loan debt.

Arnal v. Arnal, No. 26215 (South Carolina Supreme Court, October 23, 2006): A showing of "bad faith" is not necessary in order to impute income for purposes of calculating child support. The motive behind any purported reduction in income or earning capacity should be considered in determining whether an obligor parent is voluntarily underemployed, as justification for imputing income for the purposes of calculating child support, but the law does not preclude a finding of voluntary underemployment in instances where a spouse reduces his earning capacity without doing so in bad faith.

Williams v. Williams, No. COA06-284 (North Carolina Court of Appeals, October 17, 2006): Payments made by mother's father to mother via a friend for mother's vehicle and housing constituted "income:"to mother for purposes of calculating child support, and, thus, trial court was obligated to include this income in arriving at mother's child support obligation.

Meredith v. Meredith, 854 N.E.2d 942 (Indiana Court of Appeals, October 6, 2006): Evidence in post-divorce child support modification action was sufficient to support finding that father was voluntarily unemployed; father testified that he voluntarily took early retirement, testified that he was not seeking employment, and testified that he had the ability to work, but chose not to.

Oliekan v. Oliekan, 2006 UT App 405 (Utah Court of Appeals, October 5, 2006): Husband's premarital interests in basic retirement plan, deferred compensation plan, and 401k plan did not lose their identity as husband's separate property and become commingled when they were converted, cashed out, and rolled over into Individual Retirement Accounts (IRAs), and thus husband's premarital interest in plans would not be classified as marital property in divorce action, although marital and premarital funds were deposited together; it was possible to trace and separately identify marital and premarital funds.

Smith v. Smith, No. ED 86913 (Missouri Court of Appeals, Eastern District, October 3, 2006): Father was entitled to credit against his child support obligation for social security benefits received by adult disabled child due to father's disability.

In re Baker, No. 2005-380 (New Hampshire Supreme Court, September 27, 2006): Father was not entitled under child support guidelines to deduct from his gross income for purposes of calculating his support obligation for younger child the monthly payment he was making for his older child to attend college.

Gibbons v. Kugle, 2006 PA Super 264 (Pennsylvania Superior Court, September 22, 2006): Evidence supported trial court's decision requiring ex-husband to contribute to the parochial school tuition of child in proportion to his net income; parochial school tuition of $6,230.00 per year was consistent with the parties' standard of living and station in life prior to separation and, thus, was a reasonable need for child, child's parochial school tuition was consistent with ex-husband's income of $133,000, and consistent with child support guidelines, the tuition had to be allocated between the parties in proportion to their net incomes. Trial court's requiring ex-husband to contribute to a portion of his daughter's parochial school tuition did not amount to a requirement that he support a place of worship in violation of state constitutional article providing that no man can of right be compelled to attend, erect or support any place of worship.

de Leon v. Jenkins, 143 Cal. App.4th 118, 49 Cal. Rptr.3d 145 (California Court of Appeal, 4th District, September 21, 2006): Under Uniform Interstate Family Support Act (UIFSA), spouse was not precluded, by failing to object to New Mexico child support order within 25 days of its registration by county department of child support services, from challenging understatement of arrears; only non-registering party who failed to object within requisite time to "any matter that could have been asserted at time of registration" was precluding from further contesting order, and understatement of arrears was not included in statutory grounds that could have been asserted for objecting to order.

Corapcioglu v. Roosevelt, No. 1313 (Maryland Court of Special Appeals, September 20, 2006): $252,930 judgment mother obtained against father for counsel fees and costs she incurred in seeking child's return to Maryland after father had abducted child and taken him to Turkey were non-dischargeable as child support, or in the nature of child support, in context of father's bankruptcy proceeding.

Walker v. Grow, No. 2613 (Maryland Court of Special Appeals, September 12, 2006): Joining the majority of jurisdictions that have considered the issue, the court holds that retained earnings of a sub-chapter S corporation can be income for purposes of child support if the retained income are not used to fund "ordinary and necessary business-related investments." The court further held the burden is on the parent seeking to exclude pass-through income that the pass-through income is not available for child support purposes.

In re Marriage of Eilers, No. 10-05-00290-CV (Texas Court of Appeals, Waco, August 30, 2006): Trial court did not abuse its discretion by finding existence of child support contract for child who was not former husband's biological child, but of whom he took custody, and by ordering former husband to pay amount of support required by child support guidelines to fulfill his obligations under contract; power of attorney jointly executed by child's biological mother and former husband and former wife was evidence that husband and wife agreed to provide for child's financial support, husband agreed that he had signed document indicating that he was to be financially responsible for child, and wife established her right to enforce contractual obligation.

Grant v. Hager, 853 N.E.2d 167 (Indiana Court of Appeals, August 29, 2006): Under the child support guidelines, parenting time credit based on evidence that non-custodial father had children for 152 overnights, or 43% of time, could be credited towards father's weekly child support obligation and reduce obligation to zero. The Parenting Time Credit may only be applied to reduce the noncustodial parent's child support obligation to $0.00; it may not be applied to require payment of child support running from the custodial to the noncustodial parent.

In re Marriage of Anglin, No. 06-0028 (Iowa Court of Appeals, August 23, 2006): Variations in former husband's overtime compensation justified use of three-year average rather than annualized income for current year when deciding whether to modify former husband's child-support obligation; shift changes that former husband's employer had planned would reduce amount of required or available overtime. Expenses for children's dance lessons and parochial school education were not extraordinary expenses that would justify award of additional child support beyond child-support guidelines; expenses fell within contemplation of guidelines.

McKyer v. McKyer, No. COA05-810 (North Carolina Court of Appeals, August 15, 2006): Mother's receipt of $249,179.77 from the sale of the parties' marital residence did not constitute non-recurring income that had to be considered by the trial court in calculating the temporary and permanent child support, where mother was principally distributed marital the residence in the equitable distribution proceedings and was ordered to sell the residence, and the change of the asset to cash did not transform the asset to income.

Dedek v. Dedek, 851 N.E.2d 1048 (Ind. Ct. App. August 3, 2006): Father was entitled to have lump sum payment of retroactive Social Security disability benefits that children received because of his disability credited against his child support arrearage, but only for the arrearage accumulated after he filed his petition to modify his child support based on his disability.

Kimbrough v. Com., Child Support Div. ex rel. Belmar, No. 2005-CA-001532-MR (Kentucky Court of Appeals, July 21, 2006): Child support statute that provided a deduction from a parent's gross income for an "imputed child support obligation"'' for child support of prior-born children who resided with the parent had a rational basis, and thus did not violate equal protection.

In re State ex rel. Taylor, No. 2005-273 (New Hampshire Supreme Court, July 19, 2006): A lump sum personal injury settlements constitute "gross income" for purposes of child support guidelines, but the court can pro-rate the settlement over each month of remaining expected lifetime to calculate monthly support obligation.

Nelson v. Nelson, No. WD 65405 (Missouri Court of Appeals, Western District, July 11, 2006): Cost of private school expenses could be included as "other extraordinary child-rearing costs" on wife's child support worksheet and be considered by the trial court in awarding support, where wife testified that the parties' older child had an attention deficit issue and that in private school he received the attention he needed to improve his performance, and child therapist who counseled both children testified that it was in the children's best interests to remain in private schooling.

Department of Social Services v. L.T., No. 2005-CJ-1965 (Louisiana Supreme Court, July 6, 2006): Naval officer's basic allowances for housing and subsistence (BAH and BAS) were to be included in his gross income for purposes of calculating child support, although child support statute defining gross income did not specifically list BAH and BAS.

Caldwell v. State, No. S-11149 (Alaska Supreme Court, January 21, 2005): Proceeds that husband received in connection with the sale of a closely held corporation in which he held minority interest constituted one-time capital gains plus return on capital. Thus, the entire payout of his share of sales proceeds could not be treated as "income" spread evenly over a five-year period of his post-sale covenant not to compete, based on theory that non-compete provision constituted compensation for not working.

In re Marriage of Henry, No. G033727 (California Court of Appeals, Fourth District, January 28, 2005): Increased, unrealized equity value in obligor spouse's residence was improperly calculated as income in child support modification proceeding, as calculation of income of obligor spouse, who sought downward modification of child support owing to her physical disability which caused her employer to let her go, should have been limited to unemployment insurance benefits, disability insurance benefits, and any wages she had earned.

In re Marriage of Lindman, No. 2-04-0408 (Illinois Court of Appeals, Second District, January 11, 2005): Disbursements from the father's individual retirement account (IRA) constituted income for purposes of child support, and the nonrecurring nature of the father's IRA disbursements did not prevent the disbursements from bring considered as part of father's net income. Further, the father was not entitled to deduct disbursements he received from his IRA from his net income pursuant to a statute that allowed a deduction for "reasonable expenditures for the benefit of the child and other parents."

Keling v. Keling, No. ED 83915 (Missouri Court of Appeals, Eastern District, February 1, 2005): Although the wife testified she had not sought full-time work because she chose to live more frugally so she would have more time with her children, the trial court was entitled to disbelieve wife's explanation as to why she was not working full-time, and was within its discretion in imputing income of $2,427 per month to wife based upon full-time employment at $14 per hour as trained dental assistant.

Caplan v. Caplan, No. (New Jersey Supreme Court, January 28, 2005): The trial court's decision to address child support without imputing income to ex-husband, whose unearned income was sufficient to meet the reasonable needs of children, while not unreasonable, failed to give proper weight to underpinnings of child support guidelines, which were based on total income of intact family, in divorce proceeding involving high income situation; it was not fair result only to use unearned income and underlying assets to calculate support merely because income from those assets would satisfy support award.

Heselton v. Maffei, 374 N.J. Super. 184, 863 A.2d 1100 (App. Div. January 11, 2005): Payments that the ex-husband was required to make to his ex-wife as reimbursement for a bank's judgment against the ex-wife after it foreclosed on marital premises, which payments were based on ex-husband's obligation in the property settlement agreement to indemnify ex-wife from any claims arising out of the loans against the marital premises, did not constitute current alimony that was required to be taken into account when determining the parties' child support obligations.

Mateer v. Field, No. 2005 N.Y. Slip Op. 00266 (New York Appellate Division, Second Department, January 18, 2005): The parties' separation agreement, which was to be construed in accordance with laws of another state, and which obligated the father to pay for the child's college tuition and for half of her other college expenses, could not be enforced due to failure of mother and child to allow father to participate in college selection process.

Spicer v. Spicer, No. COA03-1197 (North Carolina Court of Appeals, February 2, 2005): Considering income issues, the court held: (1) the trial court properly considered husband's rent-free housing as form of gross income; (2) the definition of "income" in child support guidelines, as applied to settlements received by an obligor spouse, included awards intended to compensate obligor spouse for non-economic loss such as personal suffering and disability, and was not restricted to settlements providing compensation for lost wages; thus, the trial court properly treated principal of trust fund established for husband with proceeds from settlement as non-recurring income to husband; (3) trial court properly ordered husband to invade principal of trust fund to make lump-sum payment establishing trust for child's support.

Boumont v. Boumont, No. 20040213 (North Dakota Supreme Court, January 19, 2005): After the trial court decided to leave unchanged the equal-physical-custody provision of the divorce judgment, the court was required to apply the child support guideline concerning equal physical custody when determining whether to increase the father's child support obligation, even though actual custodial arrangement was not equal, because the guideline specifically relied on language of court orders.

Taylor v. Fezell, No. E2002-02937-SC-R11-CV (Tennessee Supreme Court, January 14, 2005): The retained earnings of a subchapter S corporation should not be imputed as income to the sole or majority stockholder unless the earnings are excessive or it is shown that the shareholder-obligor is intentionally manipulating earnings to avoid support.

Groenstein v. Groenstein, No. 04-60 (Wyoming Supreme Court, January 19, 2005): Benefits paid to child of disabled parent through Social Security Disability Insurance (SSDI) are to be included in parent's gross income when initially determining parent's child support obligation. The parent is then entitled to a credit against his/her obligation for the benefits received by the child.

[*Ed. note:* See also **Holtgrewe v. Holtgrewe**, No. ED 84274 (Missouri Court of Appeals, Eastern District, January 18, 2005), reiterating that the credit goes only to the parent whose income the benefits are given to replace.)

United States v. Morrow, 03-10085 (United States District Court, Central District of Illinois, May 6, 2005): The Deadbeat Parents Punishment Act, 18 U.S.C. § 228, violates due process by its rebuttable mandatory presumption that the existence of a court support order means the defendant has the ability to pay, by shifting to the defendant the burden of persuasion of the crime's willfulness element. The section creating the mandatory presumption, however, could be severed from remainder of statute, as the remainder of the statute was fully operative as law without the invalid section, and Congress did not intend that the two provisions must work in tandem or not at all.

Mattingly v. Mattingly, No. 2004-CA-000314-MR (Kentucky Court of Appeals, May 13, 2005): Even though the statute provides that parents are obligated for support until the child reaches age 18, when parents agree to provide college support, and the provision is incorporated into a judgment, the provision is in the nature of child support and thus non-dischargeable in bankruptcy.

D.F. v. L.T., Jr., Nos. 04-CA-1455, 04-CA-1456 (Louisiana Court of Appeals, Fifth Circuit, May 31, 2005): Breaking with the clear majority in the other states, the Louisiana court held that the father's basic allowance for subsidies and his basic allowance for housing, paid by the United States military, were not to be included in his gross income for purposes of calculating child support.

Maschoff v. Leiding, No. A04-1757 (Minnesota Court of Appeals, May 31, 2005): Parents cannot waive child support in consideration of a certain custody arrangement. They can, however, stipulate that they have equal incomes, that they have equal custody, and thus under an application of the guidelines, neither parent owes the other parent support. That's not a waiver; it's an application of the guidelines.
Abellard v. Aime, 2005 N.Y. Slip Op. 04034 (New York Appellate Division, Second Department, May 16, 2005): Monetary assistance received by the father from his own father in the form of loans was includable in the father's income for purposes of determining amount of his child support obligation.

Patrick v. Britt, No. 3992 (South Carolina Court of Appeals, May 23, 2005): Another lesson in why it's a good idea not to be a jerk in front of the judge. The court of appeals affirmed the trial court's imputation of income to the husband where he failed to provide the court with any meaningful representation of his actual income, failed to respond to the court's requests for direction with anything other than patronizing remarks, and, he testified that his personal income was $66.01 per month although his company brought in over $430,000 in gross income per month.

Chen v. Warner, No. 03-0288 (Wisconsin Supreme Court, May 6, 2005): A mother's decision to leave her employment, which paid $236,000 per year, was reasonable and she was not shirking her child support obligation, when the parties had agreed she would be available for child care, she had tried to obtain part-time employment, and she was faced with exhausting her savings without child support from the father.

Metropolitan Life Ins. Co. v. Zaldivar, No. 04-2469 (United States Court of Appeals, First Circuit, June 27, 2005): Children's claim against insured's second wife, alleging breach of decree and unjust enrichment and seeking imposition of constructive trust against policy proceeds, was preempted by Federal Employees Group Life Insurance Act (FEGLIA) which took precedence over state-court divorce decree which ordered insured to maintain life insurance policy for benefit of his children from his first marriage, since amendment to FEGLIA allowing divorce decree to govern beneficiary designation of FEGLIA policy only where copy of decree was received by employing agency before death had not occurred.

McCarthy v. Popwell, No. 2030804 (Alabama Court of Appeals, June 1, 2005): Father was not entitled to have a hypothetical amount of Social Security Disability benefits mother might receive if she applied for such benefits imputed to her, where he presented no evidence she was entitled to such benefits. Further, Social Security Survivor Benefits child received was not income to wife.

Veselsky v. Veselsky, No. S-11560 (Alaska Supreme Court, June 3, 2005): Trial court properly ordered father to be responsible for 75% of the costs of child visitation and uncovered medical expenses while wife was pursuing her master's degree, since mother's financial resources were limited while she was enrolled as a student.

Farish v. Farish, No. S05F1180 (Georgia Supreme Court, June 30, 2005): Where the father earned $10,374 per month, a high-income case, award of child support to mother of $3,000 per month for three children was appropriate.

Decker v. Decker, 829 N.E.2d 77 (Indiana Court of Appeals, June 7, 2005): The father's action providing child care for the mother, but not paying child support, did not warrant giving the father credit for non-conforming payments.

Cohen v. Cohen, No. 1993 (Maryland Court of Special Appeals, June 7, 2005): The father's voluntary contribution to his retirement plan did not have to be deducted from his gross income when establishing his child support obligation, since contribution was not a necessary business expense, he earned more than eight times more than the mother, and his contribution was more than the mother's entire yearly salary.

Burns v. Ross, 796 N.Y.S.2d 450 (New York Appellate Division, Third Department, June 9, 2005): Father's retirement benefits, consisting of a monthly payment from a lump-sum retirement payout, a supplemental income protection plan payout, and a supplemental Social Security benefit payout, were all includable as "income" in calculation of child support payments, as such payments were all reportable as taxable income on father's federal income tax return.

Brandner v. Brandner, No. 20040236 (North Dakota Supreme Court, June 22, 2005): Trial court did not err by finding that father was underemployed, for purposes of computing his child support obligation, and income should be imputed, when he had been earning $38,000 before he left his job, he testified he was living with his parents, was "helping [his] folks," and he was receiving $400 per month compensation from them, and, at time of trial, he had no plans for changing his employment situation.

Gonzalez v. Tippit, No. 03-03-00517-CV (Texas Court of Appeals, Austin, June 10, 2005): When a non-custodial parent claims as a defense to child support enforcement that the child is living with him/her, and thus support was paid directly on behalf of the child, the non-custodial parent must show that the custodial parent voluntarily relinquished actual possession and control of the child to the noncustodial parent, and the voluntary relinquishment must have been in excess of court-ordered possession and access periods, and the non-custodial parent must have provided actual support.

United States v. Venturella, 391 F.3d 120 (United States Court of Appeals, Second Circuit, December 8, 2004): For purposes of the Deadbeat Parents Act, the term "resides" in the statute prohibiting knowingly and willfully failing to pay a past due support obligation greater than $10,000 with respect to minor children residing in another state, denoted residency, rather than domicile.

N.E. v. Hedges, No. 04a0437p.06 (United States Court of Appeals, Sixth Circuit, December 4, 2004): In yet another case where a father argued that he should not have to pay child support because he did not plan the pregnancy with the mother ("His basic claim is that the mother of the child 'fraudulently induced' sexual intercourse, claiming that her birth control pills would prevent pregnancy, then left the state, married another man, and delayed seeking child support for several years after birth."), the court imposed a child support obligation, noting, "Child support has long been a tax fathers have had to pay in Western civilization." (*Ed. note:* What makes this case appalling, even more so that the fact that numerous cases have rejected these arguments, is that the father here is an attorney.)

Walters v. Weiss, 392 F.3d 306 (United States Court of Appeals, Eighth Circuit, December 17, 2004): Due process did not require the state agency responsible for collecting, distributing, and disbursing child support payments to provide more detailed information in notices accompanying support payment checks so that custodial parents could readily identify and challenge any errors in state's practices for recouping prior overpayments, inasmuch as custodial parents conceded that information being provided by state satisfied statutory and regulatory requirements, and state's interest in avoiding burdensome procedures requested by custodial parents far outweighed custodial parents' interest in avoiding risk of erroneous deprivation and probable value of requiring additional procedures.

Elsenheimer v. Elsenheimer, 22 Cal. Rptr.3d 447 (California Court of Appeals, Fourth Appellate District, Division Three, December 17, 2004): Income derived from Supplemental Security Income (SSI) benefits must be excluded from determination of parent's gross income when calculating child support, and thus noncustodial parent was not entitled to downward modification of child support order, based on custodial parent's receipt of SSI benefits.

Florida Department of Revenue v. Kaiser, No. 4D03-4038 (Florida Court of Appeals, Fourth District, December 22, 2004): Income could be imputed to father who was underemployed in a six-dollar-an-hour job as landscaper in Sarasota, where he had work experience in successfully starting and running two companies in Palm Beach County, and he chose not to reestablish the company in Palm Beach County because of the time he would spend commuting to see the children in Sarasota.

Metz v. Metz, 101 P.3d 779 (Nevada Supreme Court, December 9, 2004): Both supplement security income (SSI) and social security disability benefits (SSD) qualify as a source of a parent's gross monthly income, for the purposes of calculating the parent's child support obligation under Nevada law.

Storey v. Storey, No. A-1830-03T3 (New Jersey Superior Court, Appellate Division, December 15, 2004): Even though a husband initially lost his job due to a RIF (reduction in force), when he replaced his job as a computer specialist with a $300/week job as a massage therapist, the court could impute income because he was voluntarily underemployed.

Davis v. Davis, No. 2004 N.Y. Slip Op. 09632 (New York Appellate Division, Second Department, December 27, 2004): Income could be imputed to father who was permanently partially disabled, because he made no effort to find a job in another line of work that was not as physically demanding as his former job as a bricklayer. Thus, he was not entitled to downward modification of his child support obligation based on changed circumstances arising from his job loss.

In re Paternity of K.B., No. 2004 OK CIV APP 97 (Oklahoma Civil Appeals, Division 3, December 10, 2004): A fifteen-year-old father who was the victim of an uncharged act of criminal sexual conduct when he conceived a child with 19-year-old mother was liable to pay child support. The state's interest in requiring juvenile parents to support their children overrode its interest in protecting juveniles from improvident acts, and father was not an innocent victim since he voluntarily engaged in sexual intercourse with the mother.

Kimble v. Ellis, 101 P.3d 950 (Wyoming Supreme Court, December 10, 2004): The wife, as the custodial parent, did not have the authority to waive her right to reimbursement from ex-husband for monies spent because of the failure of the ex-husband to maintain his child support obligations, and therefore, parties' agreement wherein the ex-wife agreed to relinquish any right to pursue recovery of monies she had expended prior to the emancipation of the parties' children in exchange for a lump sum settlement was never valid and was not enforceable.

McBride v. Boughton, No. A103456 (California Court of Appeals, First District, Division 2, October 21, 2004): When an unmarried man has expended funds to support a child in reliance on the mother's representation that he is the child's father, he may not then sue the mother on an unjust enrichment theory for the return of the funds after discovering that the child is not his biological offspring.

In re Malowitz and Parr, No. 03SC439 (Colorado Supreme Court, October 4, 2004): A man's abuse and harassment of his pregnant wife, causing her to flee to Colorado from Texas, supported Colorado's exercise of long-arm jurisdiction over the man in a UIFSA action, since the man's acts "caused the child to reside in the state as a result of the acts or directives of the individual."

Tarbox v. Tarbox, No. 23723 (Connecticut Court of Appeals, August 10, 2004): Drawing a distinction between a custodial parent receiving Social Security benefits on behalf of a child and a child directly receiving those same benefits, the court held that an 18 year old's direct receipt of Social Security disability benefits on account of his father's disability cannot be credited against the father's child support obligation.

Wagner v. Wagner, 29 Fla. L. Weekly D2497 (Florida Court of Appeals, First District, November 5, 2004): Notwithstanding the choice-of-law provision in parties' marital settlement agreement, stating that agreement was to be governed by California law, the appropriate substantive law for determining whether to reduce ex-husband's child support obligation was that of Florida because the parties and their children now lived in Florida, such that Florida was the only state having a legitimate interest in the dispute.

In re Rogers, No. 97833 (Illinois Supreme Court, November 18, 2004): Gifts and "loans" that a father regularly received from his family throughout his adult life were "income" for purposes of child support.

In re Goodman, No. 115/03-1133 (Iowa Supreme Court, November 10, 2004): Where parents can be ordered to pay "necessary"educational expenses pursuant to statute, such expenses can include sorority dues and a monthly cash allowance.

Garrison v. Garrison, NO. WD63047 (Missouri Court of Appeals, Western District, November 9, 2004): Emancipation occurs when a child joins the army reserves.

Kreutzer v. Kreutzer, No. 26010 (Missouri Court of Appeals, October 29, 2004): A noncustodial mother's obligation to pay child support for her college-age daughter, an obligation imposed by statute, did not terminate with the custodial father's death and the mother becoming the de facto custodial parent.

Grettler v. Grettler, 2004 N.Y. Slip Op. 08693 (New York Appellate Division, Second Department, November 22, 2004): Father's financial circumstances were self-created due to his arrest and resulting termination of employment, and he is thus not entitled to a downward modification of child support.

Gabriel v. DiBiari, 2004 N.Y. Slip Op. 08215 (New York Appellate Division, Second Department, November 25, 2004): Income lost due to father's retirement after commencement of child support proceeding was properly imputed to him, where his claimed medical reason for retiring was uncorroborated.

Arbet v. Arbet, No. 1370 EDA 2004 (Pennsylvania Superior Court, November 15, 2004): The interest from a non-marital annuity is income for purposes of child support, as are perquisites that include health insurance, life insurance, disability insurance, pension benefits, professional development benefits, and employee services.

Drevenik v. Nardone, 2004 PA Super 434 (Pennsylvania Superior Court, November 17, 2004): Trustee for father's trust properly was directed to pay father's child support arrears from the principal and income of spendthrift trust established for father's benefit by his mother's will, as testamentary language indicated that spendthrift trust was established for "support, welfare, and education" of father, the idea of providing support in spendthrift trust, i.e., payment of daily living expenses, included all reasonable living expenses that one would occur in course of daily living, such as those involved in rearing children, and language of trust permitted use of both trust principal and income to support father's children.

Gorrell v. Harris, No. M2003-00629-COA-R3-JV (Tennessee Court of Appeals, October 15, 2004): An agreement by which the parents of a child born out of wedlock "settled" the mother's paternity and child support action for $20,000 and a release of all future claims was void as against public policy.

Case v. Case, 2004 UT App 423 (Utah Court of Appeals, November 28, 2004): Section of UIFSA that granted personal jurisdiction over non-resident respondents in child support proceedings did not apply to confer Utah with subject matter jurisdiction over petition by mother, a Utah resident, against father, a Maryland resident, to modify California divorce decree that reserved issue of child support. Long-arm statute applied only in cases where Utah had issued original order.

THE "HYDE-WOOLSEY" CHILD SUPPORT BILL

This is one of the first well-documented challenges to the child support guidelines in the printed record. The research used to support this testimony can be used by every non-custodial parent to challenge any court-imposed child support based on guidelines. This can be accomplished by a father motioning for the court to take "judicial notice" of this testimony, which is printed record, and concurrently presenting an affidavit with the individual realistic child support costs in their particular case. If the judge rejects this, the petitioner may appeal his ruling and use this testimony to support his argument in the appellate court.
**Footnotes can be searched Online via*
*http://www.deltabravo.net/cms/search.php example "fn##"***

**JOINT STATEMENT OF
DR. RICHARD WEISS and WILLIAM WOOD
DR. RICHARD WEISS IS THE DIRECTOR OF
CHILDREN'S RIGHTS COUNCIL OF ALABAMA
WILLIAM WOOD IS THE COORDINATOR FOR THE
CHILDREN'S LEGAL FOUNDATION AND THE JUSTICE
COALITION**

**H.R. 1488, THE "HYDE-WOOLSEY" CHILD SUPPORT
BILL, MARCH 16, 2000**

**WRITTEN TESTIMONY FOR THE HUMAN RESOURCES
SUBCOMMITTEE OF THE HOUSE WAYS AND MEANS
COMMITTEE**

We would like to thank the Honorable Henry Hyde and the Honorable Lynn Woolsey for this opportunity to contribute written testimony to this Committee. It is an indication of the greatness of this country when our citizenry has direct input into the National Political process. Dr. Richard Weiss is an Associate Professor of Veterinary Pathology, College of

Veterinary Medicine, Auburn University. Richard is a non-custodial parent of two daughters, 11 and 12 years old and he has recently served on several Alabama Supreme Court Committees on Custody and Divorce. William Wood is a Business Management and Technology Consultant volunteering his time to help families and children in the State of North Carolina and around the country. William is a custodial father of an 8 year-old little girl and can appreciate Ms. Woolsey's challenges in trying to raise children as a single parent.

INTRODUCTION

As is increasingly evident today, families and relationships are fragile. We have a divorce rate surpassing 50% and many of these broken marriages include children who represent our nation's next generation of leaders, scientists, doctors, lawyers, politicians, policemen, etc. More and more children find themselves in the midst of a money war, caught between feuding parents, feuding lawyers, and a state "Family" Court system who's purpose is the division of property, apportioning "visitation", awarding child support, and dissolving their parent's marriage.

Child support compliance is a 50 state plague on the United States of America with 55,000 ENFORCEMENT AGENTS. I would like to reiterate, that is 55,000 ENFORCEMENT AGENTS which does not include the police officers involved with jailing "deadbeat dads", judges, advocates, administrative personnel processing claims, OCSE staff and expenses, attorneys, (at a rough average of some $185 an hour), and other ancillary individuals and costs.
Let's consider that number for just a moment: 55,000 ENFORCEMENT AGENTS each at an estimated average salary of $25,000 a year is approximately 1.375 BILLION DOLLARS a year in just ENFORCEMENT AGENT wages

alone, excluding associated fees such as jails, courts, administrators, computer systems, lawyers, judges, and other ancillary costs associated with tracking down "deadbeat dads". Child Support collections in the United States have become BIG BUSINESS represented by special interest lobby groups offering testimony to this US House Committee. Child Support Collections in the United States has become a new millennium FEDERALLY FUNDED GROWTH INDUSTRY.

The entire industry relies on junk data and junk statistics inflated by half-truths and deceptions. These are designed to perpetuate the "deadbeat dad" myth in spite of considerable evidence that indicates more fathers are instead just "deadbroke"**fn1**.
This new growth industry constantly needs more destroyed families and children to harvest more "deadbeats" to flourish. This divorce industry seems to have now leveled off at ~50% of BROKEN FAMILIES to plunder, creating a pervasive need to recruit more "deadbeats". As a result, further distortions, fabrications, half-truths, and increasingly harsher draconian measures have been instituted to ensure greater levels of "non-compliance". The more COLLECTIONS, the fatter the "bonus check" from the Federal Government to the states and other vested interests in this new growth industry. The entire domain of Child Support Enforcement has become a haven for Junk Science by those with an interest in the destruction of the family and obsessive collection of Child Support checks.
Junk Science and Junk Data have been used to manipulate the entire lawmaking process. Peter Huber coined the phrase "junk science" to refer to questionable expert testimony in the courtroom. [fn28] "Junk science," Huber writes, "is the mirror image of real science, with much of the same form but none of the substance." [fn29] He complains that courts permit "self-styled scientists" to engage in "pseudoscientific speculation." [fn30] A central issue in the junk science debate is the

admissibility of expert opinion in the adjudicative process. [fn31]"*fn2 Though this quote deals with the courts, the entire legal process, including legislative hearings have been virtually hijacked by self-serving special interests who pretend to "protect children" but do not care what destructive side effects their advocacy may have on those children.

BACKGROUND AND CASE LAW

The Hague Convention on Recognition and Enforcement created an international cooperative in the enforcement of child support orders in 1973. "Coincidentally," in 1974 Senator Russell Long came to the conclusion that there was a connection between "fathers who abandon their children" and a growth in Aid to Families with Dependent Children (AFDC). With no study and no basis for this conclusion, his efforts led to the original federal child support and paternity legislation enacted in January 1975 *fn3. The new agency's purpose was to collect Child Support from those fathers whose children were on welfare. This was done to try to reduce welfare expenditures by funding states through their legislatures if those states would create guidelines. These "guidelines" replaced legal due process procedures for determining the actual cost of raising a child.

A landmark case occurred in the Oregon Supreme Court in 1981 that substantively explained child support doctrine *fn4. This case found that the welfare formula for Child Support Collections did not apply to cases outside of the welfare system and required a special burden of ascertaining financial details appropriate for the support of children.
It frustrated the Courts to deal with the details of determining actual needs based on gross and net income, property values, forms of compensation, and then attempting to equitably

apportion them because these cases were often appealable ***fn5**. From this original evidentiary based "rebuttable presumption" of actual costs and needs, we moved to more uniform "guidelines" presenting a facade of a rebuttable presumption (45 CFR 302) but whose outcome often prevents appeals. Today, appeals are difficult because the defining facts and specific data for the guidelines are unknown and have never been published. Therefore, the "rebuttable presumption" is only a concoction fabricated by the states to meet Federal requirements. There are, in fact, no actual costs or data available to rebut.

All of these guideline problems make the "rebuttable presumption" mandated by the Federal Government (under 45 CFR 302) a useless facade. The PSI guidelines and Income Shares exacerbate this problem by failing to meet the Federal requirement of "*the most recent economic data on child rearing costs...*" required for the stipulated quadrennial state reviews. One pending case in Alabama challenges the rebuttable presumption of the child support guidelines. ***fn6** There is a related follow up case to this that seeks to force the Courts to abide by their own contracts with Child Support awards. ***fn7** The State of Kansas has filed a Federal Appeals case against the United States Government ***fn8** and stated in opening arguments on January 20, 2000 in the 10th Circuit Court of Appeals that current Child Support guidelines are "unconstitutionally coercive".

A Michigan attorney has successfully challenged the constitutionality of some of the Child Support Enforcement practices in the State of Michigan ***fn9**. Based on this initial victory about the UNCONSTITUTIONAL nature of Michigan's practices, another Class Action has been filed representing the 2,000,000 obligors (predominantly fathers) in the state ***fn10**. The Michigan papers are beginning to recognize the Courts and the Child Support "system" are out of control ***fn11**.

In a March 1, 2000 Louisiana appeals case, the lower Court engaged in blatant, capricious, and malicious gender bias *fn12. The husband and wife had similar seasonal jobs. The husband's wages were imputed with low points of the seasonal job ignored, and the wife's wages were treated differently. The lower court's ruling was reversed on appeal. In a March 7, 2000 Minnesota appeals case *fn13, the lower court refused to correct imputed income and it too was reversed on appeal. An Ohio court of appeals remanded a case back to the lower court *fn14 on March 6, 2000 for reconsideration because Tax adjustments for the obligor were not appropriately factored into the guidelines and should have been considered as part of the "rebuttable" presumption. These are just a few of the cases heard within the last couple of months. The fact that such cases have been routinely overturned on appeal demonstrates not only that the "guidelines" are faulty but also that lower courts are reluctant to consider reasonable "rebuttals" to the guidelines. These "guidelines" have in fact become rigid de facto laws.

JUNK SCIENCE - DISTORTIONS, DECEPTIONS, DATA MANIPULATIONS, AND MISUNDERSTANDINGS

Census Bureau data from 1989 indicated that **75 percent of all child support owed is paid *fn15**, and showed that the TOTAL amount of Child Support owed was 14.8 BILLION dollars. Of that amount, 11.1 BILLION had been paid (7.6 BILLION was paid in full, and 3.5 BILLION was partially paid). According to a 1992 report by the Government Accounting Office, Child Support non-payment is NOT by choice. This report showed that 66% of the fathers were not able to pay, 5% were unable to be located, and 29% were classified as other *fn16.

Analysis of methodology used by the Census Bureau Child Support to compile data is even more disturbing. Dan Weinberg, who heads the census division that collects Child Support data, has stated that this data is **based solely on the custodial mother's recollection, and there is no cross-check or verification with the non-custodial parent OR any requirement for documentation *fn17**. This statement was made on the ABC 20/20 program on January 7, 2000, where it was concluded that "deadbeat dads" are actually "deadbroke dads". Let's reiterate, the Census Bureau data is based solely on the custodial mother's memory, influenced by her personal bias or anger, and with NO verification to support the claims. In 1992 custodial mother SELF REPORTED figures didn't quite fit the expected "deadbeat dad" outcomes ***fn18** indicating that 66% of non-support by fathers was from inability to pay. In fact, the rate of child support noncompliance by non-custodial MOTHERS is greater than that of non-custodial fathers ***fn19** yet there are no slogans about "deadbeat moms" or social ostracism.

License revocations, property liens, contempt jailing, and referrals to the US Attorney General enacted under Federal authority are not generating significantly more collections. This indicates that many targeted fathers are just "deadbroke". Simple logic dictates that revoking a license will likely result in the inability to work and therefore exacerbate the problem. "The Federal Office of Child Support Enforcement has nearly a $4 BILLION annual Budget. Of the $12 billion CS arrearages, about three-fourths of them are categorized as "uncollectable" - this is largely due to unemployment." ***fn20**

Reviewing testimony before this committee, we are now supposed to believe that some 50 BILLION dollars in Child Support is owed. That would be over 3 times the amount owed just over 10 years ago, based on inaccurate, unverified,

and likely inflated numbers (see ***fn17**). This assumption would require us to believe that any one or all of the factors underlying Child Support collections have increased by over 3 times as well: salaries have increased 3 times, divorce rates have skyrocketed 3 times, "awards" have increased 3 times, or any combination, resulting in 3 times the problem. This 50 BILLION dollar figure professed by Nick Young, Geraldine Johnson, and others testifying before this committee defies logic ***fn21**. Those with the most to gain by this system perpetuate this 50 BILLION dollar junk data figure.
US Census Bureau data indicates there are ~11.6 million custodial mothers (85% of all custody awards) collecting support. It seems a fair assumption that there are ~11.6 million Child Support obligors for an average ARREARAGE of ~$4,310. If this figure were in fact accurate, this would indicate that there are nearly 11 million obligors who are within a couple of support payments (the $5,000 threshold) of incarceration ***fn22**. With the number of states that engage in mandatory pay check withholding, this shows that either the 50 BILLION figure is false, child support "awards" are too high, or most likely, both. Will America soon require a massive penal system to house all these poor fathers?

"The Bureau of the Census reported on child support payments in the spring of 1995 ***fn23**. According to that report, the so-called "deadbeat dads" are few and far between in the population of fathers with legitimate child support orders ***fn24**. Comments on child support compliance often focus on the estimate that only about 66% of the child support that has been awarded is paid. This does not consider the fact that more than 14% of the amount under study had been recently awarded and was not yet due. Considering custodial parent reporting bias and adjusting for awards not yet due brings us closer in line with the information provided by Braver et al. ***fn25** as well as information collected by commissioners in the states. **Approximately 80% of the total amount of child support awarded in the U.S. historically has been paid each year. The compliance rate was not significantly affected by reforms." *fn26** This indicates that special interests are manufacturing a problem when none exists.

The Honorable Lynn Woolsey has stated "there were child support enforcement reform laws in 1984, 1988, 1993, and 1996. None of them resulted in any significant improvements in the rate of child support collections." ***fn27** The data would seem to indicate this is because the numbers used by those with a financial stake in Child Support Enforcement are false or misleading, and that most of the non-support is from inability to pay. To wit, a mandatory withholding experiment conducted in 10 Wisconsin counties yielded only a 2.89% increase in compliance, **INDICATING THOSE WHO COULD PAY WERE PAYING! *fn28**

Child Support enforcement has criminalized Fatherhood. ***fn29** Yet it is interesting that there is little or no information about bad mothers. If this were truly about children, there would be more public vilification of mothers based on the high rates of child abuse perpetrated solely by mothers ***fn30**. The lack of concern about children's health, safety, and welfare, coupled with the insatiable lust of the divorce industry for the FATHER'S PAYCHECK exposes the financial motivation of the entire system. Considering the US historically has had one of the highest, if not the highest, compliance rates with child support orders in the world ***fn31**, it is apparent that this system LIES about "child" support while simultaneously neglecting the welfare of children.

WHEN CHILD SUPPORT BECOMES TAX FREE ALIMONY

Robert Williams, the father of the Income Shares model, worked as a consultant with the US Health and Human Services (HHS) Office of Child Support Enforcement from 1983-1990. In 1984 he started Policy Studies, Inc. In 1987 he developed and introduced the "Income Shares" model now used by over 30 states. Williams currently consults states in Child Support guidelines while owning and operating his child support collection service with some 500 employees creating a direct conflict of interests *fn32. In the Mid 80's, under the "guise" of a need to raise child support, a 250-350% increase was suggested without specifically focusing on the child. The name of the report itself betrays the unstated motive to include Alimony or Spousal support under the pretense of increasing basic child support needs: 350%: *Estimates of National Child Support Collections Potential and the* **Income Security of Female-Headed Families *fn33**[*emphasis added*].

At about this same time (mid 80's), women's groups rallied around Lenore Weitzman's statistically flawed "73%" study in a frenzied attempt to gain alimony. This "study" with its erroneous math and questionable methods, helped disproportionately increase child support payments for the custodial parent--, ~90% of whom are mothers *fn34. This egregiously flawed data has been used in discussing child support reforms. Typically, income differences between men and women are used as an excuse for the need to increase child support. This "logic" is a direct appeal to include some form of spousal support or alimony in the "child" support calculation. Williams "model" then accepted presumed "increases" in his 1987 report.
Williams widely used Incomes Shares model is not based on separated or divorced household expenses for children, and it arbitrarily under-accounts for shared parenting time *fn35.

Standard of living adjustments aren't properly factored; Williams simply raises the numeric tables arbitrarily producing results so high that they often grossly inflate "child support" to include alimony ***fn36** (more junk "science"). Apportioning support based on time with each parent has been suggested and some judges and lawyers openly oppose these equitable determinations factoring the amount of time with each parent in child support amounts ***fn37**.

Williams (the owner of PSI) regularly advocates increasing Child Support awards with little or no credit for time with the non-custodial parent. This creates a hardship on non-custodial parents (generally fathers) struggling to remain involved with their children. This also increases the pool of potential child support obligation owed, and increased arrearage for the non-custodial father's collection division to exploit for their personal financial gain.

"Economic analysis comparing pre and post divorce standard of living is highly speculative, is based on unsubstantiated assumptions about family spending patterns, and leaves out many important considerations that would tend to show that <u>post-divorce standard of living is more nearly equal among the households of split parents</u>. ***fn38**"

Williams underlying data is flawed in its "economic" studies and information that are in fact based on non-like groups of intact families to arrive at major "statistical" conclusions ***fn39** (i.e. junk science) "*. . . the presumption that underlies the focus of much of the empirical research and policy debate on income distribution [within households] seems born of ignorance and is supported by neither theory nor fact.*" ***fn40**.

Williams' company, PSI, uses data erroneously based on the study of costs of raising children in INTACT households ***fn41**. PSI data relied partially on the Rothbarth estimator which concludes <u>family well-being depends on the amount the family spends on alcohol and tobacco!</u> ***fn42**. The Williams PSI "income shares" model also relies on the Engle estimator which is based on century-old findings of an economist, Ernst Engle. The premise appears valid at first and then Williams (PSI) extrapolates completely unrelated data from this study which dramatically inflates guideline numbers ***fn43**. Gross Income versus Net Income as well as Day care and Medical costs are estimated with no proper basis. The underlying data is erroneous and not disclosed. Most states using the Williams model also add additional amounts as separate and distinct items for daycare, health insurance, and medical expenses, yet PSI did not parse those items from the expenditures for children and are at least partially included in the base "guidelines" creating double allocations for obligors ***fn44** (all junk "science").

Some states allow for "child support" to continue AFTER a "child" is 18 and even living away from home. This comes in the form of post-secondary support for college. If a "child" is over 18, and no longer living at home, and the check is still drafted to the custodial parent and NOT the child, how can this be called "child support"?. Though supporting children through college is important, this additional burden is clearly little more than Alimony or spousal support. Ten states allow this, 11 states have restrictions, 7 are silent on the issue, and the remainder forbid it through statute or case law ***fn45**. Also, there is no accountability to the obligor for a "child" in college getting grants, loans, or other public assistance from the government.
"Robert W. Braid, an accounting, finance and economics professor, performed a detailed cost analysis in his own case in New Jersey ***fn46**. Based on a comprehensive cost and cash flow analysis, he calculated that he should pay approximately $180 per month to the mother in addition to sharing the direct

costs of education for one child in college. Based on the established New Jersey formula, he was ordered to pay $903 per month, plus half his daughter's college expenses. Mr. Braid found that the judges decision implied that it 'must cost $21,672 a year in after tax money to support one child at home full-time (excluding any medical expense and any money the father spends on vacations, entertainment and hobbies with the boy), and one child spending about 25% of her time at home and the rest in college.' "

For example, using NY income numbers shows how child support impoverishes the obligor. A non-custodial parent (father ~90% of the time), earning $55,000 per year pays child support for 2 children and ends up with an income of only $14,000. The mother, earning $26,000 per year, ends up having a disposable income of over $44,000. Tax cost of all this to American Taxpayers? Over $22 Billion! **fn47**. The cost to the obligor is virtual financial oblivion so severe that the obligor can rarely even afford an appropriate residence for maintaining a relationship with HIS children (predominantly fathers). These poor, but carefully manufactured living conditions through financial destitution are often the basis for the Courts restricting or removing even more of the father's relationship with the child.

Requirements do not exist for child support recipients to provide proof that the money was being spent in support of the children. This is clearly an "open door" to use this money for virtually any non-child related wish the custodial parent may have (alimony). The lack of accountability is violative of supporting children and promotes personal use of the "award" by the recipients **fn48**.

The press is also starting to understand that the whole "child support" shell game is about alimony or spousal support. ABC Market Watch recently did an article defining this as plainly biased against men and is by design to "hide" alimony ***fn49**. The errors and additional expenses included in the "guidelines" support the claim that there is much more than just child support included in the "award".

A fully informed challenge of the current Support "Guidelines" in effect in most states would not likely stand the reliability, validity, and methodology standards erected by the US Supreme Court for "expert" testimony. These more stringent standards recently imposed by the <u>Kumho</u> case were designed by the justices to create an affirmative responsibility by lower courts to invalidate the junk science that permeates the courts and legal system today. The Supreme Court, in a rare move declared that admitting unreliable, questionable, or invalid data was an ABUSE OF JUDICIAL DISCRETION ***fn50**. Robert Williams and his "Income Shares" model would likely not fare well in a direct, substantive, and well-prepared court challenge.

PAYING FOR THE DESTRUCTION OF OUR CHILDREN

It is finally becoming widely understood that father absence is one of the most destructive forces to children in our society --; fatherless homes account for 63% of youth suicides, 90% of all homeless and runaway children, ***fn51** 85% of all children exhibiting behavioral disorders, ***fn52** 80% of rapists motivated with displaced anger, ***fn53** 71% of all high school dropouts, ***fn54** 75% of all adolescent patients in chemical abuse centers, ***fn55** 70% of juveniles in state-operated institutions, ***fn56** and 85% of prison youths. ***fn57** Contrast this with 37.9% of fathers have no access/visitation rights ***fn58**. Non-compliance with court ordered visitation by custodial mothers prevents 77% of non-custodial fathers from being able to "visit" their children ***fn59**. Non-compliance with court ordered visitation is three times the problem of non-compliance with court ordered child support and impacts the children of divorce even more. 40% of custodial mother SELF-REPORTS indicate they interfered with the father's visitation to "punish" them, **fn60** ~50% see no value in the father's involvement with the child, **fn61** and many use the children to retaliate against the father for their own ongoing personal problems. **fn62**

The court system does not enforce orders for "visitation" but jails for non-compliance with a "child" support order. This is a clear indication that the whole DIVORCE INDUSTRY is about money and that children are just "poker chips" in this high stakes "game". Their destruction is just "collateral damage" for the marriage hating special interests pushing their junk data.

CONCLUSION

The entire arena of Family Law has become a domain of Constitutional violations and usurpation of civil rights. What a normal person would consider a Debtor's Prison has been instituted. To usurp the Constitution, the courts have "legislated" a perversion of the law declaring "contempt" as the new Debtor's Prison Mantra deceptively asserting it is not a debtor's prison because jailing for contempt can be remedied upon clearing the contempt charge (i.e. paying the DEBT! aka Debtor's Prison).

One man who earns $70 a week as a street musician is in jail now and will NOT be allowed to get out unless he can come up with $28,000 **fn63**. After all, the courts have REFUSED to allow visitation with his son for the last 6 years but DEMAND his money. Similar situations abound with the cost of the jail cell, incarceration, court time, and other fees associated for those who obviously CAN'T pay make for the state sponsored destruction and eradication of fatherhood.

A California appeals court also declared that some Child Support incarcerations were a violation of the 13th Amendment for involuntary servitude ***fn64**. Federal enforcement of Child Support through the IRS, as proposed in H.R. 1488, is arguably unconstitutional by forcing the states to comply with Title IV-D ***fn65**. The United States Supreme Court stated ***fn66**, "*Congress is without power to enlist state cooperation in a joint federal-state program by legislation which authorizes the States to violate the Equal Protection Clause.*" *and* "*[W]hile the Fifth Amendment contains no equal protection clause, it does forbid discrimination that is 'so unjustified as to be violative of due process.'* "

Nearly every state has legislation to seize bank accounts and real property without a court order (for "child" support) eliminating due process without a sworn statement that the money is owed. In child support politics, the Constitution has become passé and encumbers or impedes the cash machine that has been created. In this entire domain of "Family Law" the Constitution as we know it has ceased to exist. "*State judges, as well as federal, have the responsibility to respect and protect persons from violations of federal constitutional rights.*" ***fn67** This responsibility has been abandoned to pursue Title-IV funding for the states.

State and Federal Governments now expend HUNDREDS OF BILLIONS of dollars each year to support the marriage and family destruction INDUSTRY with little to promote or support marriage and families. There is some indication that the press is starting to take note of Child Support and the Multi-BILLION dollar Divorce INDUSTRY that destroys families and thwarts the Constitution ***fn68**. Many "deadbeat" dads are just plain "deadbroke". They are humiliated and bankrupted by a system that hides "alimony" in child support payments designed to support single mothers and their children ***fn69** making it "profitable" for women to divorce.

Under Child Support Enforcement efforts, draconian measures including "badges of infamy" like the fabled "scarlet letter" have been instituted in the form of jack boots for cars. In a Washington Times article, Nick Young has STATED the intent of such measures is humiliation *fn70.

Family Courthouses in America, in practice, have become Family slaughterhouses. Families, children, and our futures are being plundered through the use of junk science represented as '"gold standards." Destroying families and children in America has become BIG BUSINESS... A MULTI-BILLION DOLLAR INDUSTRY. The deadbeat dad myth, is just that, a myth. Fathers want accountability and equity in a system that is both unconstitutional and out of control *fn71. Fathers are being destroyed by a system that seeks to squeeze every ounce of money possible before discarding them, with abject disdain for fathers and their essential roles as nurturing parents, protectors, role models, and caretakers of their children. A father in Canada (a country with similar custody policies and child support "guidelines" as the US) recently killed himself after being ordered to pay TWICE his income in support payments *fn72. With the current junk rhetoric like the unsubstantiated 50 BILLION dollars arrearage amounts (not based on ANY FACTUAL STUDY, i.e. junk data), we are not far from this kind of tragedy being commonplace in America *fn73. This destructive DIVORCE INDUSTRY must be dismantled.

Robert Williams involvement with Child Support Guideline creation through PSI, and his Child Support Collections business creates a conflict of interest and an inherent need for his "junk science" to manufacture more "deadbeats". US citizens, as well as Federal and State governments should DEMAND A FULL REIMBURSEMENT OF ALL PUBLIC FUNDS that his Child Support Collections business has received for its destruction of families.

The IRS does not have a stellar reputation for resolving financial issues while observing the rights of the citizenry and the Child Support Guidelines are a mess. Giving them to the IRS to enforce with its dubious reputation would likely create even more of a mess ***fn74**. To resolve some of this mess and qualify for Federal Funds, the states must be required by the Federal Government to define what the child support presumptions are and then assign appropriate values to each of those presumptions to make them truly rebuttable.

The Federal Government MUST get involved, but not through Child Support Collections via the IRS. Rather, the government must now demand Justice and Equity in the state "Family" Courts, and promote the preservation of intact families by protecting the rights of children to be raised and supported--- both financially and emotionally--, by BOTH parents, even after divorce. Federally subsidized collection agencies need to stop taking from the children what their RHETORIC pretends to protect ***fn75**.

The social fabric of society is built upon the strength of its family structure. Impoverishing and vilifying parents by misguided and flawed mercenary practices of government, joined at the hip to a multi-billion dollar divorce industry, is rapidly exsanguinating and killing the American family. Restore Constitutional protections to the "Family Court" process. It's time to look past the marriage and family hating special interests, marriage hating gender politics, and the bureaucracies. Look to the families and children of America, or tomorrow there may not be an America.

FOOTNOTES

- ***fn1** BAD DADS [Dead beat vs. Dead broke dads], ABC News program 20/20, John Stossel and Barbara

Walters, January 7, 2000.

- ***fn2** Partially Quoted from 72 N.C. L. Rev. 91 at 97; "[FN28] PETER HUBER, GALILEO'S REVENGE: JUNK SCIENCE IN THE COURTROOM 2 (1991); [FN29]. Id.; [FN30]. Id. at 3. Huber notes that "[t]he best test of certainty we have is good science--the science of publication, replication, and verification, the science of consensus and peer review." Id. at 228.; [FN31]. In Daubert v. Merrell Dow Pharmaceutical Inc., 113 S. Ct. 2786 (1993), the Court dealt with the admissibility of expert testimony about scientific evidence..."
- ***fn3** The Child Support Guideline Problem, Roger F. Gay, MSc and Gregory J. Palumbo, Ph.D., May 6, 1998
- ***fn4** In the Marriage of Smith, Or 626 P2d 342 (1981).
- ***fn5** Silvia v. Silvia, 400 N.E.2d 1330
- ***fn6** Blackston v. Alabama, 30 F.3d 117. (11th Cir. 1994);
- ***fn7** U.S. District Court for the Middle District of Alabama Case # 99-A-295-N
- ***fn8** State fighting feds in appeals court, The Topeka Capital-Journal, Robert Boczkiewicz, January 22, 2000
- ***fn9** Tindall v. Wayne County Friend of the Court, 98-CV-73896-DT, Eastern District of Michigan, Southern Division; 9/30/99
- ***fn10** Child Support Collection Leads Divorced Fathers to Sue the State of Michigan, Current Events in Law - Online Section, Paul Reed, January 26, 2000
- ***fn11** Michigan Court out of Control, Wayne County FOC & Circuit Court Accused of Fraud and Abuse, Sierra Times Exclusive, Franklin Frith, February 9, 2000
- ***fn12** Otterstatter v. Otterstatter, No. 99-1481 (Louisiana Court of Appeals)
- ***fn13** Behnke v. Green-Behnke, No. C7-99-820 (Minnesota Court of Appeals)
- ***fn14** Topp v. Topp, No. 1999CA0243 (Ohio Court of Appeals, District 5): Relying on Singer v. Dickinson, 63 Ohio St. 3d 408 (1992)

- ***fn15** Current Population Reports, Series P-23, No 173, 1989
- ***fn16** GAO/HRD-92-39FS, January 9, 1992; page 19
- ***fn17** BAD DADS [Dead beat vs. Dead broke dads], ABC News program 20/20, John Stossel and Barbara Walters, January 7, 2000.
- ***fn18** GAO/HRD-92-39FS, January 9, 1992; page 19
- ***fn19** Bureau of the Census, Statistical brief - SB/95-16; June 1995
- ***fn20** Divorced Fathers: Shattering the Myths, Sanford Braver.
- ***fn21** Statement of Nick Young, Division of Child Support Enforcement; Statement of Geraldine Jensen, Association for Children for Enforcement of Support, Inc. March 16, 2000
- ***fn22** 3/99 U.S. Dept. of Commerce, Current Population Report (P60-196 Child Support For Custodial Mothers and Fathers: 1995), there are 11.6 Million Custodial Mothers (85%).
- ***fn23** Who Receives Child Support? Bureau of the Census Statistical Brief, June 1995.
- ***fn24** Although according to the data used in that report, child support had been awarded for only 56% of all separated custodial parents. Part of the lack of support orders however, can be explained by the death of an ex-spouse, agreement not requiring a court order, and other reasons. A significant part however is simply because paternity has not been established.
- ***fn25** Non-Custodial Parent's Report of Child Support Payments, Braver, Sanford, Pamela J. Fitzpatrick, and R. Curtis Bay, 1988, presented at the Symposium "Adaptation of the Non-Custodial Parent: Patterns Over Time" at the American Psychological Association Convention, Atlanta, GA, August, 1988. Compared

Bureau of Census custodial parents reports (approx. 70% received) with father survey (approx. 90% paid).

- ***fn26** The father of today's child support public policy, his personal exploitation of the system, and the fallacy of his "income shares" model, James R. Johnston, August 1998.
- ***fn27** Statement of Lynn Woolsey, M.C., CALIFORNIA, March 16, 2000.
- ***fn28** Journal of Contemporary Policy Issues, Garfinkle and Klawitter, 1992 - after instituting mandatory wage witholding of child support in Wisconsin, 10 pilot counties collected only 2.89% more of what was owed than the ten control counties that didn't garnish
- ***fn29** Beating Up on "Deadbeat Dads", American Spectator, Stephen Baskerville, August 20, 1999.
- ***fn30** Donna Shalala, "National Child Abuse Prevention Month" and Child Maltreatment 1994: Reports from the States to the National Center on Child Abuse and Neglect. Patrick Fagan, Heritage Foundation, THE CHILD ABUSE CRISIS: THE DISINTEGRATION OF MARRIAGE, FAMILY, AND THE AMERICAN COMMUNITY, Rick Thomas, The Dirty Little Secret: Abuse in Foster Care
- ***fn31** id. at footnote 25 (Non-Custodial Parent's Report of Child Support Payments)
- ***fn32** id. at footnote 25 (Non-Custodial Parent's Report of Child Support Payments)
- ***fn33** Ronald Haskins, Andrew W. Dobelstein, John S. Akin, and J. Brad Schwartz, Final Report, Office of Child Support Enforcement, April 1, 1985.

- ***fn34** The Divorce Revolution: The Unexpected Social and Economic Consequences for Women and Children in America, Lenore Weitzman, PhD, 1985. Discredited because of simple mathematical errors in her calculations and a fatally flawed methodology. She did not admit to these mistakes for 11 years until 1996 when they were openly exposed in A re-evaluation of the economic consequences of divorce. American Sociological Review 61:528-36, Peterson, R.R. 1996. As a result of Weitzman, a huge number of states - virtually all - have upwardly revised their child support guidelines by using and citing this work.
- ***fn35** The Child Support Guideline Problem, Roger F. Gay, MSc and Gregory J. Palumbo, Ph.D., May 6, 1998
- ***fn36** Gay, Roger F. The Alimony Hidden in Child Support, New Scientific Proof that Many Child Support Awards are Too High, The Children's Advocate (NJCCR, Box 316, Pluckemin, NJ 07978-0316), January, 1995, Vol. 7 No. 5.
- ***fn37** Parents Get Way to Lower Child Support, Dow Jones Newswires, Greg Winter, July 28, 1999
- ***fn38** Weitzman and Betson use the same approach to estimating pre- and post-divorce standard of living differences. Betson's paper provides a short list, including items such as visitation and tax consequences that are not included in his standard of living analysis. For a critical review of Weitzman's analysis, see the following. Abraham, Jed H., 1989, The Divorce Revolution Revisited: A Counter-Revolutionary Critique, Northern Illinois University Law Review, Vol. 9, No. 2, p. 47. (as quoted from New Equations for Calculating Child Support and Spousal Maintenance With Discussion on Child Support Guidelines, Roger Gay, July 20, 1994)

- ***fn39** The Child Support Guideline Problem, Roger F. Gay, MSc and Gregory J. Palumbo, Ph.D., May 6, 1998
- ***fn40** Allocation of Income Within the Household, Lazear, Edward P. and Robert T. Michael, University of Chicago Press, 1988.
- ***fn41** May 26, 1999 Memorandum from Richard J. Byrd, P.C. to the Virginia Quadrennial Guideline Review Panel. Analysis of the PSI Study and Recommendation. (page 1 of 13) The Panel requested this law firm to review the Guidelines and offer commentary. Richard Byrd is also the Chairman of the Family Law Section of the Fairfax Bar Association.
- ***fn42** See Footnote 40 at page 2.
- ***fn43** See Footnote 40 at page 3.
- ***fn44** See Footnote 40 at pages 5-9
- ***fn45** Allowed - CA, CT, IL, MS, MO, NJ, SC, TN, WA,WY; Restricted - AL, CO, IO (to age 22 only?), MD, MA, MI (to age 21 only?), MN, NY, OR (declared unconstitutional, under appeal), TX, UT; Silent - AR, HA, IN, NE, NV, NH, WV.
- ***fn46** The Making of a Deadbeat Dad, Robert W. Braid, Trial Lawyer, March 1993. (as quoted from New Equations for Calculating Child Support and Spousal Maintenance With Discussion on Child Support Guidelines, Roger Gay, July 20, 1994)
- ***fn47** Melanie Cummings of Children's Rights Council, illustrative Excel Spreadsheet to show the actual and real distribution of "child" support.
- ***fn48** In re Marriage of Hering, 84 Or App 360, 733 P2d 956 (1987). "the money is for the support and welfare of the children, not for the enrichment of the custodial parent."
- ***fn49** When men lose the divorce game, Courts often feel what's his is theirs, but what's hers is hers, Alan Feigenbaum, CBS Marketwatch, December 27, 1999

- ***fn50** Kumho Tire, Inc. v. Carmichael, 119 S.Ct.1167 (1999) Justice Scalia, with whom Justice O'Connor and Justice Thomas join, concurring opinion clarified stating in part "Rather, it is discretion to choose among reasonable means of excluding expertise that is fausse and science that is junky...the Daubert factors are not holy writ, in a particular case the failure to apply one or another of them may be unreasonable, and hence an abuse of discretion."
- ***fn51** U.S. D.H.H.S., Bureau of the Census
- ***fn52** Center for Disease Control
- ***fn53** Criminal Justice & Behavior, Vol 14, p. 403-26, 1978
- ***fn54** National Principals Association Report on the State of High Schools
- ***fn55** Rainbows for all God`s Children
- ***fn56** U.S. Dept. of Justice, Special Report, Sept 1988
- ***fn57** Fulton Co. Georgia jail populations, Texas Dept. of Corrections 1992
- ***fn58** p.6, col.II, para. 6, lines 4 & 5, Census Bureau P-60, #173, Sept 1991
- ***fn59** Visitational Interference - A National Study, Ms. J Annette Vanini, M.S.W. and Edward Nichols, M.S.W. (September 1992)
- ***fn60** p. 449, col. II, lines 3-6, (citing Fulton) Frequency of visitation by Divorced Fathers; Differences in Reports by Fathers and Mothers. Sanford Braver et al, Am. J. of Orthopsychiatry, 1991.
- ***fn61** Surviving the Breakup, Joan Kelly & Judith Wallerstein, p. 125
- ***fn62** Journal of Marriage & the Family, Vol. 51, p. 1015, Seltzer, Shaeffer & Charing, November 1989
- ***fn63** Man is jailed again in Child Support battle, The [New Jersey] Star Ledger, Timothy O'Conner, March 19, 2000.

- ***fn64** LLR No. 9609060.CA Moss V. Moss, September 25, 1996
- ***fn65** Blessing, Director, Arizona Department Of Economic Security v. Freestone et al. [1997, US SupCt, 95-1441]. Child Support Enforcement is not a federal right that can be used to force states to substantially comply with Title IV-D.
- ***fn66** Shapiro v. Thompson, 394 U.S. 618, 22 L.Ed.2d 600, 619, 89 S.Ct. 1322 (1969) citing Katzenbach v. Morgan, 384 U.S. 641, 651, n. 10, 16 L.Ed.2d 828, 836, 89 S.Ct. 1717 (1966) et. al.
- ***fn67** Goss v. State of Illinois, 312 F2d. 1279 (US App Ct, Illinois, 1963)
- ***fn68** Q: Is court-ordered child support doing more harm than good? Yes: This engine of the divorce industry is destroying families and the Constitution. Insight Magazine, Stephen Baskerville, Vol. 15, No. 28 -- August 2, 1999.
- ***fn69** Some 'Deadbeat' Dads Are Dead Broke, David Crary, Associated Press, November 7, 1999
- ***fn70** Pink and blue car boots shouldn't be forced on police, Police Beat - Fred Reed, The Washington Times, Jan. 10, 2000; page C2.
- ***fn71** Father's protests deserve airing, Kathleen Parker, USA Today, November 8, 1999
- ***fn72** Anti-Male Bias in Family Courts blamed for Man's Suicide, couldn't afford support payments, backers say, Donna Laframboise, National Post, March 23, 2000
- ***fn73** Throwaway Dads, Houghton Mifflin, Ross Parke and Armin Brott, 1999.
- ***fn74** Everyone Loses in the Daddy War, Wall Street Journal, Stuart Miller, May 31, 1995, page A-17.

- ***fn75** More for SRS Collections but less for Children, Kansas is taking a larger percentage of the child support payments it collects - and parents are not happy about it. Wichita Eagle, Jennifer Comes Roy, January 24, 2000

The Father's Rights Survival Guide

(Permission to reproduce here kindly given by John Phillips, Fathers -4- Justice, Canada)

The following is a comprehensive list of recommendations for men who are facing marital separation and divorce where children are involved. These recommendations are not legal advice.

They are "street smart" suggestions gleaned from personal experiences and the experiences of other men who have worked their way through the minefield that is family law.

Although the statutes stress that decisions taken in family law litigation should be, first and foremost, in "the best interests of the children", the fact is that almost all rulings are made in favor of the mother, as "primary caregiver" -- ostensibly "on behalf of" the children. As a father, you, supposedly, have rights under the law, but, quite realistically, have few rights at all. 85% of custody decisions go to the mother (mothers have custody in the vast majority of cases); mothers rarely pay child or spousal support. Fathers are routinely forced into personal bankruptcy or go underground because they cannot pay onerous support orders; mother's routinely withhold children from court-ordered 'access' with their fathers as court orders for access are virtually unenforceable; family equity is split right down the middle, even though a mother may have only provided barely adequate child care and indifferent housekeeping as her contribution. So you must take steps to preempt and mitigate, where possible, a situation wherein you are at the mercy of cut-throat lawyers, biased judges and a very flawed system.

Although the tone of this article may seem pessimistic, I propose that it is, in fact, realistic. The plight of fathers in family law disputes is grave. However, I am optimistic because of the tremendous devotion that so many fathers display for their offspring in facing overwhelming emotional and financial challenges in the simple desire to play a meaningful and critical role in their children's lives. And I sense a rising tide of awareness and anger in the general public, at large, at the inequalities and abuses of their rights that fathers have been suffering for far too long. It's time that innovative solutions like mandatory shared parenting be written into the statutes to give fathers a chance at participating in a reasonable fashion in their children's lives. Once again, it must be stressed that the following is not legal advice. Ask your lawyer/attorney for a definitive opinion on any and all of the recommendations presented here. This document is prepared specifically relative to British Columbia, Canada family law, but most principles should work relative to other North American jurisdictions.

The recommendations begin with the supposition that you are still in the matrimonial home, that your marriage is beyond saving and that mediation is not an option. If you have already separated, pick up the suggestions at the appropriate point.

1. Do not move out of the family home. If no custody order is in place, and you move out, you are granting your spouse de facto custody of your children; you immediately expose yourself to petitions for child and spousal support; you abandon all joint possessions and even your personal possessions to your spouse (and you don't have to be a lawyer to know that possession is 9/10ths of the law); and you give

your spouse leave to petition for exclusive possession of the house in perpetuity in "the best interests of the children" thus tying up the house as an asset.

2. Throughout the period of final co-habitation with your spouse, do not engage in any verbal battles..PERIOD. If the situation is volatile, do not engage in any discussions about legal or settlement issues. Do not engage in any kind of verbal or physical confrontation with her. If you do, you put yourself at the risk of her getting an order to have you thrown out of the house and possibly restrained from going anywhere near her, the property and, possibly the children. If she becomes confrontational, walk away and avoid close contact. Make the only dialogue between the two of you be about the care and well-being of the children and the day-to-day running of the home. If you simply must communicate directly to your spouse regarding matrimonial issues, do so in a written note. You can organize your thoughts better that way and avoid a verbal joust. Do not use inflammatory language, stick to the facts. Date the note and write "Without Prejudice" at the top (this protects you from later use of your note against you). And keep a copy of it for your files.

3. Throughout the period of final co-habitation with your spouse, eliminate, or at the very least, reduce, your consumption of alcohol. If you have a drug / alcohol problem, GET HELP IMMEDIATELY, otherwise you may be dead in the water. Alcohol - and most drugs – reduce your inhibitions and may make you more aggressive and thus in danger of confrontation with your spouse. And later, when you come down from your high, you will suffer from depression that will impair your ability to function and may make you susceptible to suicide. In almost all cases of murder / suicide in marital disputes, alcohol is a contributing factor.

4. If there are firearms in your home, GET RID OF THEM. Take absolutely no chances that someone may lose it and grab a gun.

5. Get emotional counseling if you need it. There is no stigma attached to getting help for the stress and the anxiety depression that almost everyone experiences during the ordeal of a high- conflict divorce. Have your family doctor recommend a psychiatrist - covered under provincial health plans in Canada (psychologists and social workers are not usually covered) – or check your employment health benefits to see if referral to a counsellor is available to employees.
If you are a member of an organized religion, your clergyman / priest / rabbi or affiliated lay counselors may provide assistance.

6. Transfer all money from joint spousal accounts to your own sole accounts. If you don't, chances are that she will clean out the accounts before you do.

7. Have your spouse's name removed from all joint credit cards for which you are responsible, get her spousal cards from her and destroy them.

8. Engage legal counsel sooner rather than later. Be prepared for the fact that you will have to provide a legal retainer of (typically) a minimum of $1,000 for a lawyer to begin working on your case. Make sure your lawyer is an experienced family law specialist, not someone who does part-time family, part-time real estate, etc. law, Ask him (or her) if he / she is aware of the bias of the family court system against fathers and if he (we'll assume it's a man from here on) is willing to fight for your rights as a parent and not be intimidated by biased court officials.

For your first meeting with him be prepared with a written outline of the issues of your case. Do not make this a novel about the emotions of your marital breakdown. Stick to the hard, cold facts. Go to all meetings with your lawyer with a written agenda, and with all issues, questions, etc. spelled out in detail. Write down all responses and action items. Be prepared to do any legwork for him that you can (document searches, brief preparations, etc.). Use his time wisely. The meter is ticking all the while you are sitting in meetings with him or consulting on the phone. And remember two things: he works for you so be demanding; and he will not (nor shouldn't) make decisions for you, you must make them yourself with his guidance.

9. Start and maintain in chronological order a comprehensive and well-organized file of ALL documents, memos, letters, briefings, affidavits pertinent to your case. Your file is critical for referring to past actions, issues, details. Take all relevant files with you for meetings with your lawyer; and take the originals plus a second set of all relevant files with you to court appearances as backup in case your lawyer does not have the appropriate ones with him.

10. Court actions. Don't even THINK about going to court without a lawyer in most cases, judges will just laugh and scoff at you literally and tell you to get representation. If you persist in forcing them to allow you to represent yourself, her lawyer and the judge will take you apart. Consult with and rely on your lawyer for the timing and the appropriateness of court actions. It may be in your best interests to get to court first with a petition or motion (to be the "petitioner"); or the other side may move quickly and make you the "respondent" to a court action.
Your lawyer should know what strategies are best. Assist him as much as you can with written briefs for the affidavits, financial statements, etc. he will prepare on your behalf.

11. Start, and maintain, throughout the duration of your case, a daily journal of all activities relative to your interaction with your spouse and the children. Memory is a faulty faculty. Being able to go to your journal to find the unfiltered facts regarding events that were written at the time of occurrence can be a critical asset.

12. Micro-manage your money. Legal fees and, inevitably, support payments will be major financial hurdles you will have to deal with. Go on an austerity budget. When you finally physically separate, you should be aware that you may be primarily responsible for financing two households. Start a war chest of any and all money you can squirrel away. Line up resources for borrowing because, eventually, you are going to have to solicit loans.

13. Be prepared for the "equalization of family assets". This means that, even though your spouse may not have worked outside the house a day in her life (her parenting and housekeeping are her contribution to the marriage), in general, she is due 50% of all the assets accumulated during the marriage. That is, in general: she gets half the proceeds of the sale of the house and properties, half the RRSP savings, half the investments, half the family liquid assets, half your employment pension, half the value of all vehicles and half the furnishings, etc. of the home accumulated during the marriage. If she works, all her assets including RRSPs and pensions she may have accumulated -- will be included in the division of assets.

14. A note about the "separation date": This is a critical date for figuring out the equalization of assets. In general, you both keep whatever assets you brought to the marriage. However, all assets accumulated between from the "date of marriage"

until the "separation date" are split 50/50. The separation date is typically the date that one of you leaves the matrimonial home. The status of that date may change if the one who left returns for any amount of time. A separation date may be established while you are still together. Usually, it's the date that you stop sleeping together in the same room, but may require the added proviso that you have stopped doing things together as a family.

15. Be prepared to not get any form of custody of your children. In general, at the present time, if you go to court in dispute over custody of the children, say you want joint custody and she wants sole custody. The biased judges in the family law system will rule that: "since you two are in dispute over the custody arrangement, joint custody will not work. Therefore "in the best interests of the children", the primary caretaker of the children (guess who?) will have sole custody of the children." In general, the only way you will ever get joint custody is if she agrees to it; the only way you will ever get sole custody is if she does not want custody at all or you can prove that she is completely unfit and incompetent to be the custodial parent (and you will have to have comprehensive and incontrovertible evidence). There are cases of enlightened judges granting joint custody when there is a dispute, however, it is a very rare exception.

16. Be prepared to pay child support. Because you will not get joint custody of your children in a contested case, you will automatically be ordered to pay full child support for all children of the marriage, common-law relationship (or proven paternity situation).

The support order in Canada is based solely on your gross income and the number of your children relative to tables provided by the government. And it will be enforced by the enforcement branch of your provincial government if you default on payments. Once the order is registered, the support amount will be automatically collected from you by a government agency and paid to your ex -- unless you both agree to opt out of the plan and make arrangements for you to pay her directly. You may also be liable for a percentage of childcare expenses, based on the inequity of your salaries, if your ex is gainfully employed. And you are liable for other "reasonable" extra expenses, i.e.: medical, dental, schooling, sports activities, etc.

17. Be prepared to pay spousal support. If your wife is a homemaker, you will be required to pay "spousal support" until such time as she can become gainfully employed. Some judges put a time frame to spousal support giving the wife a period of one year, etc. to find / return to work. In some cases, where the wife has never worked and is at home with small children, you may be liable for spousal support for quite some time. If your wife is a part-time employee or "under-employed" you may be required to provide an equalizing amount of support relative to your income and hers. The fact that women, typically, make less money than men means there may be an equalization of income by way of spousal support. There are no tables for spousal support.
The lawyers and the judge will work out an amount and you will be ordered to pay it.

18. Pay your support orders when humanly possible. You have an obligation to financially support your children even if you believe the order for support was unreasonably arrived at. If you do not pay your support, the money will be garnisheed from your wages at source and your savings and RRSPs, etc. will be seized. You will get yourself into very serious financial straits if you let the ordered amounts accumulate over the years. And you will be hounded forever by the enforcement office. If your income declines, go back to

court and petition for a reduction in support. But pay the support as ordered until you get the amount reduced. Do not withhold child support if your spouse is interfering with your time with the children. The courts treat child support and access as two completely separate issues. And they are. If you withhold child support, you are engaging in the same dirty tactics that she is. And the children are the ones who suffer. And you look like the bad guy. And you can't afford to look like the bad guy, given the existing bias against you as a father.

19. Be prepared to fight for "access" with your children. When you don't get custody status with your children, you will be required to petition for regular visitation or access time with your children. The terms "access" and "visitation" are demeaning to non-custodial parents ("family time with the children", although long, would be a better term.), however they are the terms used in the family courts. Depending on your circumstances: job responsibilities, other personal obligations, etc. you will figure out how much time you wish to have with your children. It may be several weekday evenings and one of the weekend days with overnights, etc. Whatever your petition, be prepared for the majority of judges in the family court system to rule in favour of the mother's suggestions for your time with the children, invariably much less time than you want.

Typically, rulings are for the father to have the children every second weekend. Every other weekend is not nearly enough time to maintain the bonds you have developed with your children, but you will have to make the best of a bad deal. If the mother does not want you to have overnight visitation, you can be sure, in general, that you won't get it. Once you have an order for access in place, you can be sure that the mother's control freak nature will surface and she will find all kinds of excuses to withhold the children from you on a regular basis. And, even though she may be in contempt of a court order, don't waste your money taking her to court. A judge will almost never penalize her in any meaningful way for her actions, except, maybe, to lecture her (is anyone going to fine or throw a mother of children into jail?). Keep a record of all the withheld access visits and have your lawyer lodge official protests that may be used, cumulatively as proof of her contempt at later court appearances.

20. If you have been cut off from seeing your children because of malicious and false allegations of abuse: Take the unusual step of petitioning for "supervised access" at a centre provided by your local or provincial government. There would have to be tremendous extenuating circumstances for a judge to deny this kind of petition. Even though the circumstance of spending time with your children under supervision will be stressful and humiliating, it will ensure that you have regular contact with them. And, in the meantime, you can pursue having a "family assessment" by an appropriate professional to disprove the allegations.

21. Malicious and false allegations of child sexual abuse have become an insidious phenomenon in family law. A 1998 report by the Ottawa Ontario Children's Aid Society revealed that, of 900 cases of allegations of child sexual abuse linked to matrimonial disputes, 600 of them were proved to be completely groundless. Meanwhile the victims of this devastating weapon (fathers fighting for meaningful relationships with their children) are required to PROVE their innocence.

The custody / access issue grinds to a halt as the Children's Aid, the police and psychiatric professionals involve themselves in an already crowded process. Access between the father and his children is severely curtailed or terminated and the emotional and financial costs of an already painful process escalate. The perpetrator of this gross injustice (the mother, usually by prompting the children) faces no recrimination or penalty for her actions. And the relationship between the father and his children is severely strained or, all too often, irreversibly damaged.

22. Family assessments have become a growth industry. With all the malicious allegations flying, courts routinely order "family assessments" to be conducted by social workers and psychologists who have trained as experts in this area of the family law industry. They interview all relevant parties and then come back with findings and recommendations that are usually accepted by the judge who ordered it. These professionals have to be paid; and guess who usually gets stuck with that bill? Often when a family assessment has been ordered, you at least get to suggest a candidate for the job. Make sure you propose someone who is at least impartial about, if not outright sympathetic to, fathers' issues. And lean on your lawyer to be forthright in the decision-making for the assessor.

23. Face the fact that you may have to endure a very long period of frustrations and disappointments. The processes of the court system are slow enough and frustrating enough on their own. Then there are the lawyers. In collusion with their intransigent clients, they are masters at delaying and frustrating court actions. They conveniently and consistently "miss phone calls", ignore messages, "miscommunicate" and "misunderstand"; disappear on holidays; ask for continuances (delays in proceedings), all with the intention of frustrating you from getting court actions completed that they may feel are not in their client's interest. And the judges: it is so unnerving to go before a judge, as a taxpayer, sound citizen

and devoted father and to be regarded by this "god in his kingdom" as a second-class (at best) citizen, a wannabe parent and a bottomless pit of financial resources. And, on the other hand, treating your wife as the only trustworthy, sane, long-suffering puritan in view. Patience and persistence is the only thing that will get you through, guys. Patience and persistence.

24. Maintain lines of communication with your children. LISTEN TO THEM. Let them express their fears and concerns and hurts. Reassure them, as much as you can. Prepare for your time with them. Line up activities: bowling, a movie, etc.; have the fridge stocked with their favorite meals (from lists you can have them prepare). Don't just let them plunk down in front of the
TV and order in fast food (although that's what they may demand). Get them outside participating in sports and physical activities, walking by a lake or stream, visiting favorite relatives (don't forget Gramma and Grandpa!). Avoid shopping, even grocery shopping with them. Your finances will be strained and you don't need the pressure they will bring to bear on you to buy them "things". Instead, listen and watch for a special item they may be yearning for and, where practical, buy it for them as a surprise gift. Make sure you buy something for each child, though.

25. Do not trash talk your ex in front of the children. Even if you are aware that she puts you down in their presence. The children love you both equally and your criticisms of one another will only confuse them and stress them even more than they already are. In the long run, it is counterproductive for either parent to put down the other. Eventually - and it may be a long way down the road - the children will see through the criticisms and lies and will turn against the trash-

talking parent. And never argue about aspects of the case or any other issue in front of them. This will just make them more anxious and angry about their new fractured life situation.

26. Keep in touch with your children through any channel possible when you see them very little or not at all. Write to them, send them cards and little gifts, telephone them, send them emails.

Keep a record / copies of the things you send if you suspect your ex is intercepting your correspondences and the children are not getting them. Somewhere down the road, you can show your child proof of your efforts to keep in touch. And they are going to know that it wasn't your lack of interest in being part of their lives, but their mom's interference.

27. Throughout the ordeal of the divorce process, rely on your spiritual path be it Christian, Jewish, Muslim, Buddhist to help you get through.
Attend your church, synagogue, temple on a regular basis. Find some quiet time for reflection and meditation, to drop right out of your ordeal and renew your soul and spirit.

28. Don't be too proud, as a man, to rely on your friends and family for emotional support. Don't think that you have to carry the often overwhelming burden of the injustices and the stresses of your case by yourself. Your friends and family, who love you, will usually be there to share the weight of the ordeal. WARNING: realize that, even though your family and friends can lend a sympathetic ear, they can also get overwhelmed by your case if you go on about it too much. Don't be a broken record; use their sympathy wisely. And let your friends periodically entertain and distract you to help you relieve yourself of the seriousness of your circumstances.

29. Help others in similar circumstances and join the fight for Fathers' Rights. Be generous with your time and advice with fellow victims of the sham of so-called "family" law. Write letters to newspapers, your elected representatives, the governing bodies for judges and lawyers. Join a father's rights organization and picket and protest the inequities in court decisions. It will take serious and concerted efforts by all of us to bring about the changes that are needed in the true application of the principles of family law.

30. Get regular exercise and eat well. Try to jog or participate in sports on a regular basis. Avoid the grease and salt and sugar of fast food. Take the time and care to feed yourself nutritious and healthy foods. It bears repeating here: eat lots of fresh fruit and vegetables; have good amounts of whole grain breads and cereals; eat lean cuts of red meat, poultry and fish. Make sure you go for your yearly physical.

31. Get yourself a pet, preferably a dog. There's nothing like the unconditional love and affection of a faithful pet when you return home from work at the end of an exhausting day. That wagging tail, affectionate gaze and total lack of attitude can do wonders for you. And the walk it will demand every night will be good for your mind and body too.

32. Be easy on yourself. You are going to feel like a failure: a failure in marriage, a failure to your children, a financial failure. Accept responsibility for the role you played in the debacle, but DON'T BEAT YOURSELF UP OVER IT. About the perceived failure of your relationship with your wife: realize that "incompatibility is like rain: it just happens." Realize that your children need your emotional support, so give yourself a break: be easy-going and affectionate with them.

Realize that you walked into a financial minefield when you entered the domain of family law.

Unless you started off filthy rich, you are going to take a financial pounding, and it ain't your fault. Try to not let it stress you out.

33. Last point: Women are not the enemy. Just because your wife turned out to be your worst nightmare; and just because family law is completely biased in favour of mothers - even mothers from Hell; don't get down on the "fairer sex". Family law has swung so far askew because of the extreme and consistent lobbying efforts of feminist organizations and because of the overt actions of feminist-sympathizing politicians. However, your mother, your sister, your female friends, your new partner are all as appalled as you are at the injustice of it all. And they stand by to help and support and nurture you in your fight for fairness for you and your children.

The History of Child Support in the United States

When?	What?	Information
Pre-19th Century	The poor laws from 1601	The earliest history of child support in the USA came from the inheritance of the English poor laws. These laws were intended to allow parishes (local communities) to recover their costs of keeping people out of destitution from the relatives of those people. The laws didn't allow those people themselves (or other people) to claim from their relatives.
Pre-1776	Child support in the 13 colonies	"Child support law existed in the thirteen colonies and has existed in the states since the beginning of the nation's history". **Gay**.
See below: about 1800 to 1880	Development of civil law for child support	See **Hansen**. At first, courts developed civil law for child support. This especially enabled communities that kept lone mothers and children out of destitution to claim from the fathers. (This was

		similar in principle to the poor laws, but intended to be clearer and more effective).
1808	Stanton v. Willson Connecticut	
1816	Van Valkinburgh v. Watson New York	"American courts in the nineteenth century addressed the problem of dependency among single mothers and their children by creating a legally enforceable child support duty.... One reason for the divergent fortunes of men and women after a divorce was that the transformations in the American conception of children from wage earners to dependents who needed constant nurturing and the trend toward maternal preference in custody decisions combined to require divorced women to bear the burden of raising children who did not work.... American courts in the nineteenth century invented a parental child support obligation in the context of increasing concerns about dependency among single mothers...."
1858	Tomkins v. Tomkins New Jersey	

When single motherhood began to emerge in nineteenth-century America, the judiciary was the only institution of the American state that could deal with dependency among single mothers and their children: The poor laws were being overwhelmed by population growth and urbanization, and private charities and state poor-relief agencies had not yet appeared. The first child support statutes built on this judicial innovation, codifying a child support system that relied primarily on payments from absent parents, instead of on public supports for families." **Hansen**.

| See below: about 1870 onward | Development of criminal law for failing to support children | See **Hansen**. Now states started to pass laws against desertion and nonsupport. It started to become a criminal offence, with punishments including prison. Also, gradually it became possible for individuals, such as lone mothers, to |

		claim child support.
By 1886	(Compilation of statutes)	By 1886, 11 states had made it a penal offence for a father to abandon or refuse to support his minor children. Typically, it still needed evidence that without this support the children would be a cost to the community. **Hansen**.
1884 1897 1903	New Jersey statute Bowen v. State Ohio State v. Peabody Rhode Island	Examples of states taking action because fathers were criminally responsible for allowing children to become a public charge. The New York statute punished non-supporting fathers with imprisonment and hard labor. **Hansen**.
1st half of 20th Century		The court system continued to operate. The number of separated families continued to rise. 46 states had laws criminalizing desertion and non-support.
1935	**Social Security Act of 1935 (Public Law 74-271)**	This included Aid for Dependent Children. ADC (later AFDC; F = Families) established a partnership between the federal government and the states

by providing appropriations to those states which adopted plans approved by the Secretary of Health and Human Services. The states in turn provided a minimum monthly subsistence payment to families meeting established need requirements (such as an absent parent not providing support). This later gradually drove child support enforcement, in order to reduce expenditure on AFDC (see events below).

"Care for children" becomes one of the few entitlements for welfare. Compared with other countries, this tends to make "child support by parents" a prominent objective.

World War 2

2nd half of 20th Century and onwards	USA becomes unique in not having state-provided universal family allowances	"In most industrialized nations, private child support payments are not a central way in which the community makes sure that children are adequately supported. Instead, most

industrialized nations have some kind of child allowances financed by the public or by employers that go to all families. In England, for instance, families receive a universal "Child Benefit" to defray the costs of raising children; and all single-parent families receive an additional "One Parent Benefit". But although the United States has generous, publicly funded benefits such as Social Security and Medicare for elderly Americans, no comparable program exists for children.... A privatized child support system might have been a background factor that lessened the pressure for family allowances in early-twentieth-century America." **Hansen**.

1948	The Uniform Enforcement of Foreign Judgments Act (UEFJA)	Some limited applicability to child support, and largely replaced by the 1964 version.
1950	Uniform Reciprocal Enforcement of	This act has been enacted in all 50 States, the District of

	Support Act (URESA)	Columbia, Guam, Puerto Rico, and the Virgin Islands. The purpose of URESA was to provide a system for the interstate enforcement of support orders without requiring the person seeking support to go (or have her legal representative go) to the State in which the noncustodial parent resided. Where the URESA provisions between the two States are compatible, the law can be used to establish paternity, locate an absent parent, and establish, modify, or enforce a support order across State lines.
1950	Social Security Act Amendments of 1950 (Public Law 81-734)	The law required state welfare agencies to notify law enforcement officials when providing AFDC to a child. (Presumably, local officials would then undertake to locate nonresident parents and make them pay child support). The Uniform Reciprocal Enforcement of Support

		Act (URESA) was approved. (See above).
1952	Amendment to URESA 1950	
1958	Amendment to URESA 1950	
1964	The Uniform Enforcement of Foreign Judgments Act (UEFJA)	Implemented by most states and DC. Some relevance to child support orders.
1965	Social Security Amendments of 1965 (Public Law 89-97)	Allowed welfare agencies to obtain addresses and employers of obligated parents from the U.S. Department of Health, Education and Welfare.
1967	Social Security Amendments of 1967 (Public Law 90-248)	Allowed states access to IRS for addresses of obligated parents. Each state was required to establish a single child support unit for AFDC children. States were required to work cooperatively.
1968	Revision to URESA (RURESA) 1950	(Revised Uniform Reciprocal Enforcement of Support Act).

1973	Uniform Parentage Act 1973	Rules for the presumption of parentage, etc. Only adopted by a minority of states. Should be replaced by the 2000 Act.
1974 - 1975	Social Security Amendments of 1974 (Public Law 93-647) (Child Support and Establishment of Paternity Program)	A response by Congress to reduce public expenditures on welfare by obtaining support from noncustodial parents on an ongoing basis, to help non-AFDC families get support so they could stay off public assistance, and to establish paternity for children born outside marriage so child support could be obtained for them. Mandated that the State plan for child support require States to cooperate with other States in establishing paternity, locating absent parents, and securing compliance with court orders. Created (commencing January 1975) Title IV-D of the Social Security Act, the child support program. The program was designed for cost recovery of state and federal outlays on public assistance and for cost avoidance to help families

leave welfare and to help families avoid turning to public assistance. This statute, as amended, authorizes Federal matching funds to be used for enforcing support obligations by locating nonresident parents, establishing paternity, establishing child support awards, and collecting child support payments. This established the basis of the CSES. It required every State to establish a child support enforcement system. States had to establish special agencies for the collection of child support payments due to recipients of AFDC who were required to sign over to the state claims to child support as a condition of eligibility. States were required to offer similar services to non-AFDC cases if requested.

| 1976 | (Public Law 94-566) | *Title V: Miscellaneous Provisions*: Requires that upon request of a public agency administering or supervising the |

		administration of a State plan approved under title IV (Grants to States for Aid and Services to Needy Families with Children) of the Social Security Act, shall furnish to such agency making the request, information with respect to unemployment compensation, and refusal by an individual to accept employment. (Required state employment agencies to provide addresses of obligated parents to state child support agencies).
1977	(Public Law 95-30)	Amended section 454 of the Social Security Act relating to the garnishment of a federal employee's wages for child support.
1980	Social Security Disability Amendments of 1980 (Public Law 86-265)	Provided state and local child support agencies access to wage information held by the Social Security Administration and state employment agencies for establishing and enforcing child support obligations.
1981	Omnibus Reconciliation Act	1) IRS was authorized to withhold tax refunds for

	of 1981 (Public Law 97-35)	delinquent child support; 2) IV-D agencies were required to collect spousal support for AFDC families; 3) IV-D agencies were required to collect fees from parents delinquent in child support; 4) obligations assigned to the state were no longer dischargeable in bankruptcy proceedings; and 5) states were required to withhold a portion of unemployment for delinquent support
1984	Child Support Amendments of 1984 (Public Law 98-378) (Mandated guidelines to be used in an advisory capacity).	Section 3 of the 1984 Child Support Enforcement Amendments required every State's child support enforcement agency to establish procedures for automatically withholding income from the pay and tax refunds of absentee parents, whenever their child support payments fell into arrears of over one month, without having to request court intervention. It also required States to establish procedures imposing: "lines against

real and personal property for the amount of overdue support ... [and] Permitted states to extend withholding to income other then wages, such as bonuses and commissions, or dividends."

Additionally, Sections 15 and 18 required States to establish a committee responsible for formulating child support award guidelines. Once established these were to be provided to: "all judges and other officials who have the power to determine child support awards within such State, but need not be binding".

Required States to limit the role of the courts significantly by implementing administrative or judicial expedited processes. States are required to have quasi-judicial or administrative systems to expedite the process for obtaining and enforcing a support order.

| 1986 | Omnibus Budget Reconciliation Act | Required States to treat past due support |

	of 1986 (Public Law 99-509)	obligations as final judgments entitled to full faith and credit in every State. Thus, a person who has a support order in one State does not have to obtain a second order in another State to obtain the money due should the debtor parent move from the issuing court's jurisdiction. The second State can modify the order prospectively if it finds that circumstances exist to justify a change, but the second State may not retroactively modify a child support order.
1987	Uniform Marriage and Divorce Act 1987	(Adopted by a minority of states). Requires that child support be based in part on the financial resources of both parents and in part on the standard of living the child would have enjoyed had the marriage not been dissolved.
1987	Omnibus Budget Reconciliation Act of 1987 (Public Law 100-203)	Required states to provide services to families with an absent parent who receives Medicaid and have them assign their support rights

		to the state.
1988	1988 Family Support Act (Public Law 100-485)	Title I of the 1988 FSA implemented a national Child Support Enforcement System based upon the uniform application of a State-developed formula to ensure absent parents were held responsible for maintaining their children. Section 101 requires every State to implement various procedures for immediate and mandatory wage-withholding for all support orders being enforced by the State's CSEA. This law required the appointment of an Assistant Secretary for Family Support within DHHS (Department of Health and Human Services) to administer the Child Support Enforcement Program. Mandated that by 1994, states implement presumptive, rather than advisory, guidelines. Enacted "immediate" wage withholding.
1990	Omnibus Budget	Permanently extended the

	Reconciliation Act 1990 (Public Law 101-508)	federal provision that allows states to ask the Internal Revenue Service to deduct child support arrears of at least US$500 from tax refunds to non-custodial parents.
1992	Child Support Recovery Act of 1992 (Public Law 102-521)	Imposed a Federal criminal penalty for the willful failure to pay a past due child support obligation to a child who resides in another State and that has remained unpaid for longer than a year or is greater than $5,000. For the first conviction, the penalty is a fine of up to $5,000, imprisonment for not more than 6 months, or both; for a second conviction, the penalty is a fine of not more than $250,000, imprisonment for up to 2 years, or both.
1992	Uniform Interstate Family Support Act (UIFSA)	It is designed to deal with desertion and nonsupport by instituting uniform laws in all 50 States and the District of Columbia. The core of UIFSA is limiting control of a child support case to a single State,

		thereby ensuring that only one child support order from one court or child support agency is in effect at any given time.
1993	Omnibus Budget Reconciliation Act of 1993 (Public Law 103-66)	Required states to establish paternity on 75 percent of the children in their caseload instead of 50 percent. States had to adopt civil procedures for voluntary acknowledgement of paternity. The law also required states to adopt laws to ensure the medical compliance in orders.
1994	Bankruptcy Reform Act 1994 (Public Law 103-394)	Protected child support from being discharged in bankruptcy. It also provided protection against trustee avoidance, facilitates access to bankruptcy proceedings, and assigns child support a priority for collecting claims from debtors.
1994	Full Faith and Credit for Child Support Orders Act of 1994 (Public Law	This is binding in all the states and supercedes any inconsistent provisions of state law. It restricts a State

	103-383)	court's ability to modify a child support order issued by another State unless the child and the custodial parent have moved to the State where the modification is sought or have agreed to the modification.
1994	Work and Responsibility Act of 1994	Included assisting states with child support enforcement.
1994	Small Business Administration Amendments of 1994 (Public Law 103-403)	Renders delinquent child support payers ineligible for small business loans.
1994	Social Security Act Amendments of 1994 (Public Law 103-432)	Requires states to periodically report debtor parents to consumer reporting agencies.
1996	**Personal Responsibility and Work Opportunity Reconciliation Act (PRWORA) of 1996 (Public Law 104-193)** (Welfare reform law)	Under the new law, each State must operate a CSE Program meeting Federal requirements in order to be eligible for TANF funds (which replaced AFDC). This law made about 50 changes to the CSE Program, many of them major. These changes

included requiring States to increase the percentage of fathers identified, establishing an integrated, automated network linking all States to information about the location and assets of parents, requiring States to implement more enforcement techniques, and revising the rules governing the distribution of past due (arrearage) child support payments to former recipients of public assistance.

Under the new law, states can implement tough child support enforcement techniques such as withholding wages, seizing assets, and revoking driving and professional licenses of those parents who owe child support. Set aside 1 percent of the Federal share of retained child support collections for information dissemination and technical assistance to States (including technical assistance related to automated systems), training of State and Federal staff, staffing studies, and related activities needed to improve the CSE Program, and research, demonstration, and special projects of regional or national significance relating to the operation of the CSE Program. An additional 2 percent of the Federal share of retained child support collections is set aside for the operation of the Federal Parent Locator Service (FPLS). Expanded the scope of the FPLS to allow certain noncustodial parents to obtain information regarding the location of the custodial parent. Streamlines the paternity determination process. Required all States to enact UIFSA (see below), including all amendments, before January 1, 1998 Increased its access to information and maintaining its effort to automate caseload processing. The legislation mandated that states require employers to report all new hires within 20 days to child support enforcement authorities. This new requirement was expected to reduce the delay in establishing immediate wage withholding.

PRWORA also eliminated the federal requirement that states pass through the first $50 of child support paid to welfare families.

| 1996 | **Uniform Interstate Family Support Act (UIFSA) (1996)** | The Uniform Interstate Family Support Act ("UIFSA") was drafted to more efficiently enforce the child and spousal support orders as well as paternity judgments of other states and countries. The prerequisite to enforce another country's orders under UIFSA is that the country of origin must have a "law or procedure substantially similar to UIFSA's, or one of UIFSA's precursors -- the Uniform Reciprocal Enforcement of Support Act ("URESA") and the Revised Uniform Reciprocal Enforcement of |

		Support Act ("RURESA").
1997	Balanced Budget Act of 1997 (Public Law 105-33)	Allows FPLS (Federal Parent Locator Service) information to be disclosed to noncustodial parents except in cases where there is evidence of domestic violence or child abuse and the local court determines that disclosure may result in harm to the custodial parent or child.
1998	Child Support Performance and Incentive Act of 1998 (Public Law 105-200)	Provides penalties for failure to meet data processing requirements, reforms incentive payments, and provides penalties for violating inter-jurisdictional adoption requirements. Incentive payments are based on paternity establishment, order establishment, current support collected, cases paying past due support, and cost effectiveness and on a percentage of collections. Incentive payments must be reinvested in the state's child support program.
1998	Deadbeat Parents	The law establishes two

	Punishment Act of 1998 (Public Law 105-187)	new categories of felony offenses, subject to a 2-year maximum prison term. The offenses are: (1) traveling in interstate or foreign commerce with the intent to evade a support obligation if the obligation has remained unpaid for more than 1 year or is greater than $5,000; and (2) willfully failing to pay a child support obligation regarding a child residing in another State if the obligation has remained unpaid for more than 2 years or is greater than $10,000.
1998	Bradley Amendment (*42 USC* Sec. *666*)	The Bradley Amendment prohibits judges from retroactively modifying child support.
2000	**Uniform Parentage Act 2000**	This has been drafted in the hope that states will enact it and become more uniform in their approach to parentage, and especially paternity. Among other things, it emphasizes genetic testing, but also recognizes the strength of acknowledgement of

paternity. **Morgan**.

| 2002-12-12 | **Australia and the United States entered into a treaty for reciprocal recognition and enforcement of child support maintenance arrangements**. | This new treaty allows administrative assessments made under the Australian Child Support Scheme to be recognised and enforced in the United States. Another feature of the treaty is that each country will have a central authority which will take responsibility for coordinating all agencies involved in a case. In Australia's case, that central authority will be the Child Support Registrar. |

References

Hansen: "**The American invention of child support: dependency and punishment in early American child support law**".
Yale Law Journal, Hansen, Drew D. 1999 (March)
Morgan: **Child Support Guidelines: Interpretation and Application**
Laura W. Morgan
Ways & Means: The 2000 House Ways and Means
Green Book, "Child Support Enforcement Program"
Washington State: Washington State, Department of Social and Health Services
Child Support Federal Legislative History

GAO: **Child Support - an uncertain income supplement for families leaving welfare (US)**
GAO/HEHS-98-168 Child Support and Time-Limited Welfare, August 1998
United States General Accounting Office
Gay: **A Return to Welfare As We Knew It? The beginning of the end of child support reform**